Spirit Lives!

DR. JOHN B. MUCIACCIA

AUTHOR'S PREFACE

The main purpose of *Spirit Lives!* is to illustrate the fact that life goes on after physical death. The many voices echoed throughout its pages lift us from the darkness of the unknown, speaking with the authority and knowledge that only first hand experiences provide. Some may view them as foolish hope or wishful thinking, but hope is based on a "maybe," whereas the unquestionable existence of life after death is at the heart of this book.

The knowledge that life continues after physical death can be healing in innumerable ways, as in the case of those who endlessly wonder why their existence goes on while the life of a devoted family member or dear friend has ended. The stories contained here bring a wider range of possibilities to those who believe that death is the end, and to those who feel this worldly life is the one and only life there is. It can ignite a spark for those who have lost all hope in surviving and going beyond present existence.

Spirit Lives! also aims at planting the seed of eternal life in the consciousness of many who live with the emotional devastation of losing a loved one and mourn to the point of losing their way — seeds of the belief that this marvelous thing we call "life" is much more than what we might have been taught. And, sharing this reality, we also realize that we are much more than we might have been led to believe. There is a Oneness to all of life and each and every one of us is part of that Oneness.

The book is composed of narratives collected from both ordinary everyday people who have had extraordinary experiences and from many professional channelers, mediums, and psychics who have made communicating with the spirits of the physically dead their life's work. The stories reveal how the extraordinary is truly the ordinary to those who delve into Spirit.

Spirit Lives! overflowed in and through me, crying out to be recorded and shared with the many who starve for the light of understanding and the knowledge that our souls go on living when we are physically finished with our lives on Earth.

It outlines how, at an early age, I realized that my maternal grandfather knew things before they happened, and how that gift or ability intrigued me for the rest of my life. I chronicle how, as an eighteen year old teenager, I discovered mediums and direct contact with spirits, and detail how I began to practice meditations aimed at finding a connection to my own father fifteen years after he had passed. The joy that I find in that connection is something I want to share with everyone in order to let them know that reaching their loved ones is not only possible, but also healing to the whole of our being.

It is my belief that there is only one side, and that those considered to be on the "other side" are still on this side, waiting for a connection to be made. The notion of an "other side" only serves to keep Spirit at a non-communicative distance from us. That assumed separation does not exist. There is no separation between the physically living and the physically dead. The physically dead are in a new and different consciousness, but they are still very much alive and eager to communicate.

Spirit Lives! is not a book about religion even though certain specific religions are mentioned in some of its stories. It goes above and beyond any religion since Spirit precedes all religions and, therefore, needs no interpretation, which is the ultimate function of religion. Spirit needs no introduction, no filter through which it must be viewed. Mahatma Gandhi said it best, "Truth is one, paths are many." Simply stated, Spirit is.

With these ideas in mind, let us enter the world of Spirit through the prism of these stories. The world of Spirit is a fascinating, glorious, and welcoming place to observe. Welcoming because our friends and loved ones want us to connect with them. Step forward into this world of wonder and allow the seed to grow!

ACKNOWLEDGEMENTS

My most deeply felt thanks go to Roger Ansanelli, Mark Scardigno, Rafi Cordova, Marie Stella Cordova, Ashley Newton, Maurico Bradshaw, Chris Vanore, Joe Brennan, Cathy Grato King, Ray King, Lois Grato, Nick & Olga Calabrese, Ciara Calabrese, Alan deVelasco, Bob Richter, Mary Calabrese O'Reilly, Carmella Giambona, Wendye Chaitin, Nady Kwait, Michael Cioffi, Timothy Regan, Fred Puglisi, Mary Beth Schmelz-Weber, Pegi Schmelz-DeMeo, Luis Vidal, Enid Woodbine Maishman, Karen Schmelz-Timpanaro, and to all my friends and relatives in Spirit.

DEDICATION

To Our Friends and Relatives in Spirit

TABLE OF CONTENTS

INTRODUCTION:
MY FATHER AND MY PROCESS

Several years ago, I was in a session with a spiritual counselor discussing an emotional problem confronting me. At one point, I asked him a question and he replied, "Why don't you ask your father?" In disbelief, I said, "My father died several years ago! How in the world can I ask him anything?" With a smile on his face, the counselor gently said, "Your father might have physically died several years ago, but he lives fully in Spirit. Ask him your question. He can answer you. He wants to answer you directly."

Unbeknownst to me, that was the beginning of a very personal dialogue with my father in Spirit. Every night, for the next few years, I would "go" to my father with questions and an open mind to hear whatever advice he had to give. Over time, he has offered uncannily accurate answers to my questions. But, to fully understand this unlikely dialogue, one must know the background of both my relationship with my father and the family dynamics that surrounded it.

My father's name was Frank Muciaccia. He worked as a dental technician at the Stowe & Eddy laboratories in New York City — the largest in the United States, and Mom, Betty, stayed at home fulfilling her role as a post World War II American homemaker. In 1957, Mom and Dad had the opportunity to buy the house where we lived, and two years later, my sister got married and left to start her own family.

In 1988, my mother passed away after a challenging time with heart disease and lung cancer. At the time, Dad was 88 and in excellent health. Since I occupied an apartment in the same house, I had remained very close to both of my parents. During the years between Mom's death and Dad's passing, I established an even stronger bond with my father, one that has lasted well past his physical death in 1993.

My father was hospitalized for the last 29 days of his life due to a broken shoulder, and passed away on February 5 due to complications from the injury. It had become my practice to visit Dad twice a day, first at 6 a.m. before going to work, and then around 5 p.m. so I could spend time with him during the dinner hour. I continued this pattern every day, without exception.

On the afternoon of February 5, I entered the hospital and, as was my custom in passing the nurses' station, asked the head nurse how Dad had spent the day. She replied that he had had a good day, but something, perhaps my intuition or a sense of knowing, made me disbelieve her. When I entered his room, I immediately knew Dad was not well. He was in bed, barely moving, and his mouth had a "Q" shape to it. I approached him and intuitively realized that he wanted to make his transition. My first words to him were, "Dad, do you want to go?" He looked at me, but could not speak.

Standing to his left, I softly told him that if he wanted to go it would be with my approval and blessings. I told him that Mom would be waiting for him and that I was going to be fine. I went on to say that his own mother, father, and sisters would be waiting as well to lovingly embrace him and welcome him to Spirit. Furthermore, I told him that everything I had ever read or heard about death was that it was a wonderful and peaceful experience. All through this, the "Q" shape, which medical authorities describe as the look on a patient's face just before death, persisted.

A minute or two before his transition, I said to him, "Dad, the last words I want you to hear are that I love you," and, within seconds, he peacefully stopped breathing. Even though I knew he had died, I did not call out for the nurse or the house physician to resuscitate him. Dad had lived a beautiful life and his passing was dignified, peaceful, and natural. I am honored to have been there with him.

During the following 90 minutes, I continued to talk to Dad, speaking out loud as though he were still physically alive. Everything I had read and learned told me that, after death, the body needed to be allowed to remain still and peaceful, so that the soul could make a calm exit. I was intent on having Dad be at peace at that time.

In those 90 minutes, I also shaved his two-day-old beard, as odd as that may sound. It had been my practice to shave him every other day while he was hospitalized and the day he passed was a "shave day" for him. I lathered his face and shaved him lovingly and carefully, all the while talking to him. I told him that he had been a great, respected man both to me and to the whole family. I did not find speaking to him unusual at all because I could still feel his presence and knew that he was alive and listening in Spirit. We had a warm, loving conversation in which I did all the talking. I did not cry, but had a special sense of peace in that he had allowed me to assist him in his transition.

I removed the shoulder sling he had been wearing and dressed him in his own pajamas, then I walked out to the nurses' station, and softly, almost whispering, told the nurse on duty that Dad had passed. She immediately came into the room, placed her stethoscope to his chest, and began to cry. She later told me that Dad had reminded her of her own father. For me, it was a wonderful testimony of the gentleman my father had been, and of how loved he had been by so many.

Wiping back tears, the nurse called in the house physician to pronounce Dad legally dead. He did his duty and told me that the body would have to be moved to the hospital morgue to await the funeral director's arrival. I asked him if I would be allowed to help take Dad's body to the morgue and he agreed without hesitation.

At Dad's funeral, I delivered the eulogy to a room full of friends, family, and Hoboken dentists. I made note of what a wonderful, peaceful man Dad had been and thanked the mourners for attending. Since I had decided not to have Dad's body brought to a church — he was never a churchgoer — a priest came to perform a blessing. His blessing and my eulogy were all the ceremony I deemed appropriate in this instance.

Dad survived six and a half years after Mom's passing and during those years we were very close. In fact, I was a lifeline for him and this fostered a loving relationship between us. Because we lived in the same building, I was able to see him every day and be his caregiver. This time we shared gave me the knowledge that love connections forged on Earth are eternal and that love would continue when Dad passed to Spirit.

You can now better appreciate how surprising and meaningful it was for me to hear my spiritual counselor say that I should go to my father with my questions. Well, I took him at his word, and soon was following the daily practice he suggested — a simple, easy process of mediation.

Meditation is supposed to be effortless, and the way I choose to do it is very straightforward. I pick a time of day, either early in the morning as soon as I wake up or late at night just before bedtime, and prepare myself emotionally. These are what I like to call "quiet times," since the world has either not yet awakened or is ready to go to sleep.

Some people, I am sure, can meditate in the middle of Times Square at rush hour. I, however, cannot do that. I like to meditate in the same place and at the same time every day. For me, it is just before bedtime at my dining room table with the lights turned low, but not completely off. I sit in a straight-backed chair, light a white candle, and have a 3" x 5" index card and a pen in front of me; ready to write down any message I receive. A piece of advice, do not rely on memory! I have found that it is much better to write down everything you receive, so that you can read it at any point in the future. Deep meditations can have the same quality of dreams and if you do not record them, you are likely to forget the information received once you return to your normal non-meditative state of consciousness.

I begin my meditation sessions with a couple of prayers (any prayers will do) to calm my mind, and then I relax for a while before asking the first question. With this short process, I ask my father's spirit to be with me and to counsel me in areas of my life where I might need guidance. Actually, this method has proven so effective, that I usually begin to get messages even before I light the candle! When I ask a question, I listen for a direct answer to that specific question. If the answer appears unclear, vague, or in any way general, I pose the question again and ask for a clearer response. Most of the times though, the answers are question specific.

Even after years of connecting to my father's essence in this way, I still experience a sense of awe at the quality of the guidance I receive. Dad's advice can be mind-boggling in its accuracy and specificity. The world of Spirit is limitless and ever prepared to help us in our journey through life.

Paramahansa Yogananda presents a concise idea of meditation in his brilliantly written book *The Law of Success*. He tells us that, "All successful men and women devote much time to deep concentration. They are able to dive deeply within their minds to find the pearls of right solutions for the problems that confront them. If you learn how to withdraw your attention from all objects of distraction and to place it upon one object of concentration, you, too, will know how to attract at will whatever you need."

More specifically, Yogananda advises, "Before embarking on important undertakings, sit quietly, calm your senses and thoughts, and meditate deeply. You will then be guided by the great creative power of Spirit. After that, you should utilize all necessary material means to achieve your goal." Yogananda instructs us to be simple and effortless in our meditation. Anyone can meditate; it is easy and natural.

Before we proceed to the main body of the book, I must address a very important question. You may wonder why I am so certain that the spirit with whom I connect is in fact the spirit of my father. I recognize that consciousness as the essence of my father's spirit because of the tone and the energy of the answers it provides — they are absolutely my dad's. After all, wouldn't a son recognize his own father? Also, the things he knows can only come from him and his intimate knowledge of me. Furthermore, at an emotional level, the love I feel when I contact him during meditation is the same love I experienced all through my life from my loving father.

Consciousness lives on in Spirit after the physical body disintegrates on Earth, I have no doubt about that. It is an energy that allows for communication and it is eternal. In many ways, the spiritual world is livelier and more animated than the world of the physical where things are finite and perceptions limited.

PART I

MY OWN EXPERIENCES

MY FIRST CONTACTS WITH SPIRIT

Ever since childhood, I have been fascinated with people who demonstrate spiritual gifts like clairvoyance and mediumship. As a young boy, and because of my Italian background, I was surrounded by a belief system that supported the notion of a spirit world. In fact, it was widely known that my maternal grandfather, Giuseppe Galioto, was blessed by Spirit, and would know certain things before they happened. I grew up believing that some people were just gifted that way and could do things like predict future events and communicate with the spirits of the dead. After all, my grandfather could do it, so why not others?

Then, one day during the summer after my freshman year in college, I read an article in my hometown newspaper about a gifted psychic who had helped many families in their search for missing loved ones. Her name was Florence Sternfels. Many of the cases she consulted on involved kidnapped and murdered children with desperate families looking to find out what had happened to them. I was particularly moved by these stories and clearly saw how Mrs. Sternfels was using her psychic gifts in the service of humanity.

Local police departments would bring Mrs. Sternfels in to consult on these cases because she possessed a special sensitivity for situations involving missing or abducted children. She was the loving "grandmother psychic" who wanted to help resolve these horrendous situations, and was deeply involved and concerned with every single case she accepted.

The article went on to mention that Mrs. Sternfels lived in Edgewater, New Jersey, about five miles from Hoboken, my hometown. One evening, being the ever-curious teenager, I borrowed the family car and drove the five miles to Mrs. Sternfels's home. I vividly remember parking my car in front of her house at what was then known as 67 State Road, walking over to the entrance, and ringing the bell. A frail, elderly woman greeted me at the door. The way she looked gave the impression of someone recuperating from an illness. I would later learn that she had undergone open-heart surgery not long before my visit.

Little did I know, as I rang the bell, that the experience I was about to have would further lay the foundation for writing this book so many years later — another indication that everything is connected and that there is no such thing as a coincidence.

I introduced myself as an interested person who had read the newspaper article about her. Mrs. Sternfels acted as though our meeting had been pre-arranged and significant. She graciously welcomed me into her home and could not have been nicer in doing so. After all, I was a stranger without an appointment.

I was intrigued to be in the home of such an internationally famous person. Although it felt like a few minutes, I spent over an hour talking to Mrs. Sternfels about her work. She carefully explained what she did and how she did it, taking her time with her explanations. She told me that she mostly worked with psychometry — feeling and interpreting the energy emanating from objects. It was her gift and she was proud of it. She told me how her abilities had first manifested and why she had dedicated her life to helping others. One day, she had been innocently holding a piece of clothing belonging to a friend, when, all of a sudden, she had started to receive "communications" from the seemingly insignificant object. The story of the person came forth through the energy in the clothing.

After our talk, she invited me to return a few days later when she would be having a group reading. Mrs. Sternfels explained that she opened her home on Sunday evenings to anyone who wanted to be read or ask a question. She did not charge any money and usually had a good turnout. I agreed and left Mrs. Sternfels's home with the wonderful anticipation of returning the following Sunday.

Back home, I began to count the hours until I would return to Mrs. Sternfels's for the group reading. I called my best friend, Joe, told him about my experience, and thinking that I might want company to help me understand the group reading, asked him if he wanted to go with me — he eagerly said yes.

A few days later, we were off to Mrs. Sternfels's. As we drove, I discovered that Joe was a bonafide skeptic about all matters relating to psychics and the paranormal. I was happy to hear this because his skepticism would be a good counter-balance to my enthusiasm. All Joe talked about on the ride to Edgewater was that he thought we were entering an area of speculation and nothing more. He had only come to keep me company.

When we arrived, I could feel a buzz inside. As we stepped into the living room, there were at least thirty people already gathered there. The small living room where I had chatted with Mrs. Sternfels just a few days earlier was now crammed with people in eager anticipation.

Most of the people looked like they were regulars to Mrs. Sternfels's Sunday gatherings, and they all seemed to know each other. It appeared that this was the place to be in Edgewater on Sunday evenings! The group readings were open to anybody who wanted to attend, and there was never even a donation cup at the door. Free meant free to Florence Sternfels. She had a gift and was more than willing to share it with any truth seeker who might come knocking; this explained why I was so warmly welcomed a few nights earlier.

The gathering lasted about three hours. Mrs. Sternfels would go around the room and identify people by pointing her finger in their direction. She would then give answers to both their spoken and unspoken questions. It was amazing to witness how shocked participants were to see their mental questions answered without the need to verbalize them. Her finger pointing appeared to be random as she went around the room with her gaze.

If you had a question about someone who was not present at the evening gathering, you could bring an item that belonged to that person. Acceptable items were a piece of clothing, jewelry, or a photo of the absent person. Mrs. Sternfels worked with psychometry picking up the energy of that person from the object. A photograph was an excellent tool for her. She would pick up energy patterns and give such accurate readings that the evening was full of "oh's" and "ah's."

One could tell from the reactions of the people that the questions were being answered accurately. The whole group was obviously excited by the experience. There was not a single dissatisfied or uninterested participant in the house — the energy was palpable!

Joe and I sat amid this throng of excited people, and within the first hour, she pointed at him and immediately described, almost word for word, the conversation we had had in the car on the ride up from Hoboken. "You are a skeptic, and don't believe in the spiritual world," she said gently, but firmly. Joe turned to me and whispered incredulously, "How did she know that?" That was all she said to him, but it seemed that she was glad to have a skeptic come to her readings. The experience could serve as a good opportunity to open his eyes to the world of spirit; it gave her a glimmer of hope that he might have some sort of awakening.

When she got to me some minutes later, her remarks were softer, "You will do very well when you complete school and you will be successful... and, don't forget that!" Then she added, "Always think good thoughts." I have never forgotten those words.

All throughout the readings, she continually referred to friends and relatives who were in Spirit. She asked those present to identify the particular individual who was answering a question through her. It was impressive to watch and hear what this grandmother psychic said to her audience.

By the time the readings were completed, Joe and I had watched every person in the room receive some sort of answer to their questions. This included the handful of people who had brought photos or personal items of their loved ones who were either too ill to attend or were missing. Mrs. Sternfels read for everyone. As I look back on that experience, I realize that part of her special gift was to give encouragement. Even Joe received encouragement through what happened in that living room. Florence Sternfels was a living angel to those who came under her influence.

Recently, I met a lovely lady named Marie Christiansen, who has been living in Edgewater since 1955. Mrs. Christiansen was neither a friend nor a client of Mrs. Sternfels's, but she remembers seeing large crowds outside Mrs. Sternfels's home on the evenings when Mrs. Sternfels would give readings. Mrs. Christiansen was an eyewitness to the "draw" that Florence Sternfels had and remembers that people came from all over to be read by this gifted woman.

Mrs. Sternfels passed away about two years after I met her. In addition to the article I read in my local newspaper, she was also featured in newspapers and magazines around the world. *Parade* magazine featured her in their April 1964 issue, as did the *The New York Times*. She was well respected for all the help she had given grieving families over the years.

The ride back home was an animated one as Joe and I talked about what we had just seen and heard. It would be safe to say that he went from being a skeptic to a believer in the course of the three hours we spent in the company of

Florence Sternfels. He had experienced a sort of conversion; a conversion that has affected him for the rest of his life.

I became stronger in my convictions of the existence of a "world beyond" as real as the physical world of our daily experience. Maybe the world out there was even more real because it was direct, honest, and contained no energy for lies and intrigue. Through my experiences with my grandfather and with Florence Sternfels, these convictions had been so established that by the time I was eighteen there was no doubt in my mind about the reality of Spirit. The succeeding years only continued to prove that a spiritual life awaits us, and that we may die physically, but live on fully in Spirit as close to the physically living as a breath of air.

I GO TO MY FATHER EVERY NIGHT

My own journey into the realm of Spirit has been nothing less than amazing. Whatever Hollywood concocts in its most spectacular movies cannot hold a candle to the plots Spirit weaves in our daily lives. The millions of events through which people, places, and things interact, the endless combinations that manifest life, and the "coincidences" that rule men's destinies are way beyond human comprehension.

All of us know trials and tribulations from hard fought life experiences, and, as M. Scott Peck writes in *The Road Less Traveled*, "life is difficult" and "life is a series of problems." He also quotes one of the Buddha's most famous declarations, "Life is suffering." Having all these thoughts in our consciousness, we can either call it quits or we can choose to endure life's difficulties and problems by looking at them through the eyes of Spirit.

By going to my father every night, I have chosen the latter. I have seen too many people jump head first into difficulties without paying any thought to either the spiritual origin of an issue or its possible spiritual solution. After a while, you would think their heads would hurt from following the same strategy every time they face a challenge. There is no amount of aspirin that can alleviate a head that keeps on butting up against the immovable object that is life. A few years ago, I decided to take an easier road by following my spiritual counselor's advice and going to my father's spirit for guidance. "Why don't you ask your father?" my counselor said. It was that question, and my response to it, that led me to the material that prompted the creation of this book.

From the very first session of communing with my father in Spirit, something made me keep a record of our dialogue. I wrote down every answer I received. My intention was never that of writing a book, as a matter of fact, when I began recording my father's comments, I had no idea that someday they would form part of one.

Right from the beginning, I asked him probing questions about our special connection. I wanted to know more about the process through which he was able to answer my seemingly endless questions. One day, I said, "Dad, how do you do what you do? How do you manage to have answers to all my questions?" His reply, "You ask the question of all questions when you wonder what my source is. The spiritual world is so different from anything a human could understand. It is an all-knowing universe where everything is mind and little to nothing takes place in the physical. When we need to know something all we have to do is think of it. When we want to see someone all we need to do is picture the person. There are no negative emotions here, no jealousy, anger, fear, contempt, avarice or anything else you could think of and experience in the earthly physical world.

Perhaps this is why humans refer to this sphere of existence as heaven — a place without physical or emotional pain. In doing so, they are using their intuition correctly. There is no want or need because the soul resides in a spiritual world where it needs no food, drink, clothing, housing, cars, schooling, relationships, or any of the earthly desires.

We are the source of all information and need only think of a question to have an instant response; the right answer is always at our immediate disposal. Our source is what you refer to as the Creator; the creative force behind all that is.

Rest assured that when you ask a human question, we see the situation from an elevated perspective and are eager to give you answers that will prevent unnecessary suffering in the human plane. Suffering is something we do not enjoy seeing in any human entity. We want you to be right and happy."

The answer was staggering, but I knew he spoke the truth because of the many specific questions I had asked and the many detailed and accurate answers I had received. Dad also added that many times Spirit gives a type of "group answer" to a question or a prayer. Spirit knows, beyond all human comprehension, the appropriate course of action, and the perfect way to present it.

Humans, in our arrogance, think we know the source of all things, but our level of ignorance far outweighs our information. This is why past life regression and near death experience accounts are filled with such awe and astonishment when souls cross over and begin to describe what they actually see on the other side. Many therapists must coax their patients to use human vocabulary to describe spiritual scenes since doing so can prove a formidable challenge.

You must keep in mind that any and all topics are open for discussion when you engage in this type of meditation work; Spirit does not shy away from any subject. Personal life, health, happiness, marital relations, education, business, human relationships, sexuality, and romance are all grist for the mill when you connect with Spirit. I look upon these conversations as conversations with a best and trusted friend.

ADVICE FROM DAD

When I began connecting with my father's spirit, I was in the midst of a dispute with some tenants. I had realized, much to my dismay, that a few months earlier, I had rented the apartment on the top floor of my building to a couple that displayed the most immature of behaviors. I live on the first two floors of the brownstone, so this couple's drama was playing itself out right on top of my life. From the day they moved into the building, I could sense there was going to be trouble. They were party people and had no regard for other people's comfort.

The couple had apparently asked six of their friends to help them move with the promise of free beer, but it all indicated that the beer party had begun way before the move. The scene was set for disaster, eight amateur movers under the influence of alcohol and a moving truck loaded with heavy furniture.

By the end of the day, damages to the hallways tallied up to a thousand dollars. The walls, banisters, floors, ceiling, and the dead bolt on the front door were all scratched, broken, or otherwise destroyed. Plaster dust ruled the day covering every available inch of carpeting. Midnight found me staring up at the ceiling with what turned out to be the first of many parties in full swing right above my head.

Neither the male nor the female of the couple ever acknowledged the situation. They acted as though they were completely unaware of the damage they and their friends had incurred while in their drunken state.

The weekend was only two days away, so another house party must have already been on their schedule. This one lasted until 4 am when I declared it over whether they liked it or not. I had been very close to calling the police on my tenants of three days, but thought I would give them yet another chance.

When the second party was quickly followed by a third the following evening, I knew there was a serious problem inside my house. I, however, had no idea how to solve it since there was the not so minor detail of a signed one-year lease. When I went to my father that night, he said, "Don't fret over upstairs. The more you fret the worse it becomes due to the energy you create." That sage advice was followed by, "We are with you now, we are always with you."

I was even more heartened by his next words, "Know it is taken care of." I had the feeling that it would be taken care of quickly. "The girl upstairs is angry, but it is not your concern. Let her be angry, he has to deal with it, not you." Furthermore, "Good people are coming in after them."

He told me to... "pause during the day, in your car or at lunch at work and call me to you"; supporting words I so needed at that point in my life.

When times were trying during this landlord-tenant dispute, I was told, "You have never been abandoned, although you mistakenly believe so." Additionally, "Things are going beautifully for you and will be getting even more beautiful. Have an open mind, heart, and attitude." In the face of this disturbing situation, I was given strength and the promise of hope.

I began to visualize these tenants moving out. I pictured the man knocking on my door and asking if they could break the lease. I would then see myself asking him in to go over the details of doing so. I would visualize this scene clearly, in minute detail, and within a few weeks, my tenant came knocking at my door asking for permission to break the lease.

My first experience of direct contact with Spirit through the essence of my father gave me the comfort and the strength necessary to get through this situation unruffled. This would be the first of many life challenges that Spirit would guide me through and help me interpret in a positive light.

Once the unruly tenants moved out, I had a realtor show the apartment. One of the first people to come see it was a man named Bob. His first reaction was non-committal, but Spirit told me that he would be back in a few days and rent the apartment. Spirit assured me that Bob would be a good replacement for those who had left.

The apartment was vacant a month or two, but then Bob came back and has been living there ever since. He is a quiet, perfect gentleman who keeps to himself and has never done anything to disturb the peace inside the home.

Shortly thereafter, I had to deal with a long-term friend who was being emotionally destructive both to himself and to those around him. He was morbidly obese, finding his only source of love and relief in his addiction to food. I did not know how to help him, but again, I was not alone. Through a series of meditations, I learned that this friend was simply unable to hear what I, or anyone else, had to say. Spirit answered my queries with the metaphysical lesson, "do your best and leave the rest."

Relationship issues of all types often came up during this time. I received great insights that led the people I was doing business with and me into win-win situations. This is one of the great advantages of working with Spirit — Spirit wants to see everyone win. The fact that I was the one meditating did not mean that they would want to see me and only me succeed.

At this time, a group of my South Korean students were spearheading an initiative that would have me move to Seoul in order to teach English, but, although the thought was intriguing to me, dialogues with Sprit presented the opportunity as a sign that my business was expanding rather than as a call for me to move to Seoul.

A friend was presenting herself as troubled and insecure, more like a wounded child than a balanced middle-aged woman. Spirit counseled me to visualize her as a three-year old child and to lovingly take her along with me during my daily routine — in the house, walking next to me, and riding in my car every day. The visualizations worked like a charm. In no time, she started to moderate her behavior and began liking herself more. Once again, a win-win situation had been produced in front of my very eyes.

For years, I was the exclusive in-house English tutor at Southpole, a prosperous Korean owned clothing manufacturing company in Fort Lee, New Jersey. Occasionally, I had questions about text book selection or methodology, and Dad never failed in making remarkable educational recommendations that benefited my students and helped me become a more sensitive teacher.

Through my nightly conversations with him, I also learned to see people and things from a clearer perspective. Very often, people's words and actions are incongruous, and I had not been very keen at seeing this.

In the spring of 2009, I suffered temporary nerve damage to one of my fingers on account of an errant needle in the hands of my acupuncturist. I was concerned that the damage would be permanent, but Dad continually stressed that the doctor who had caused the problem would also be able to make it heal. That is exactly what happened resulting in my complete recovery.

How Spirit is able to orchestrate this universal dance is a marvel for any mortal to behold. Spirit guides and supports us, and we are all able to connect to it. It is a story that unfolds precisely as it was meant to unfold for the harmony contained within the experience.

Self-esteem and self-confidence have always been an integral theme in my conversations with Dad. Old topics would also come up for clarification without me calling attention to them. It was almost as though his spirit knew what or who needed support. His "random" comments would sometimes surprise me, but they were always well timed and honored.

At one point, the readings took on a rather interesting bent when Dad said, "You are on the threshold of a new and happy life. Take hold and grasp it with gratitude." As usual, Dad's prediction was impeccably timed since I happened to be at a juncture where I needed some excitement and encouragement injected into my life.

In many cases, I was told that experiences were planned for me in order to facilitate my journey. At these moments, I felt even more respect for the spiritual world and what goes on beyond our understanding. I would hear, "All is good" and would then be able to proceed confidently.

At one point, I was advised, "This is the calm before the abundance!" Spirit went on to say, "Your life is coming into its own;" beautifully motivating words for me to receive.

The fact that I needed to accept my abundance was presented to me many times. It is common for humans to be fearful when abundance hits them in the face. I was being taught how to lovingly embrace all that was headed into my life and to accept that I was prepared and happy.

At one point, I had a conflict with a contractor who was supposed to do work in my house. The advice I received from Dad was to see the man clearly for who he was and to forgive and forget about him. It was a lesson in dealing with conflict; some people are unreasonable and must be forgiven.

"I am always with you. We are working on your case now. Ask me for anything." These words brought with them the transformative energy of Spirit, and situations would shift and change for the better. Supreme intelligence knows everything and acts without having to be asked.

My father was able to quickly and decisively diagnose all sorts of maladies — sinus infections, insomnia, aches and pains of all sorts, headaches, and other ailments — without any type of hesitancy or error. The ability to offer remedies was part of Spirit's wisdom, as well.

At one point, I met a lady named Young, and I could not figure out why I had drawn her into my life. When I asked Dad, he replied that it was for me to learn how to cultivate a friendship with a woman without the involvement of romance. I thought that was fascinating because, according to this woman's story, she had never had a romantic relationship with a man.

My relationship to Spirit has also made me keenly aware of different energies and energy fields, some of which are good for me to be in and embody, and some that need purging. Some people, for example, are destined to come into our energy fields and us into theirs for the purpose of cleansing. At the time these people leave, we must let them go because all involved have already been served, and there would be no further need for them to remain in our lives or us in theirs.

In the late summer of 2009, I prepared to spend a few days in Banff, Alberta, Canada. I planned to stay at the Fairmount Banff Springs Hotel located inside the Banff National Park amid the Canadian Rocky Mountains. Spirit told me that I would feel a presence while in Banff, and that the energy there would be exactly what I needed to experience.

While in Banff, I had what I refer to as my "Waiter Dream." Interpreted by Spirit, it was a dream that expressed my feelings of inadequacy in the face of abundance. It came to make me aware of these feelings and to help me release the patterns of unworthiness, so that I would be able to receive all the abundance heading my way. The clear message was, "Accept, accept, accept. Whatever offer is given to you, accept."

Back at Southpole, in the autumn of 2009, the HR department met with me to discuss the cancellation of the ESL program. Due to dire financial circumstances and the state of the national economy, the company had no choice, but to enact cost-saving measures. Following Dad's advice, I grew greater than the situation and responded with pure gratitude for all the years I had been allowed to teach there. There was not a trace of anger or disappointment in me. That night, the message I received was, "It is always darkest before the dawn.

Remember that and know the dawn is coming beautifully. Allow the Southpole situation to take place, as it must. If the door closes, and it probably will, a wider, bigger, and better door will open for you!" The Southpole ESL program concluded in November 2009. As I look back, I realize that the ending of my tenure at Southpole facilitated my transition into becoming a full-time writer. It opened the time and the space for me to be able to concentrate on my writing career and complete my first book, *Thinking In English,* before the end of the following year.

During one session, Dad said, "Your mom is here with me. You may ask her questions, too." Mom talked about how strong her union was with my father and that my future mate, whom she already knew in Spirit, wanted ours to be as strong, too. The notion of "believe and see" came up a few times.

Very often the readings talked about the energy change that occurs as a result of a certain thing happening. For example, going on a vacation, such as the one to Banff, had helped to change my energy patterns. I was led to that destination specifically because it would have just that effect on me, and make me ready for a particular experience coming my way.

At one point in the autumn of 2009, I took a road trip to Stockbridge, Massachusetts, known for its beautiful foliage. A few days before leaving, Dad said, "The trip to Stockbridge is about energy. Like a fill-up at a gas station, this will be a positive energy fill-up for the abundance and for the relationship you will have with a woman."

In November 2009, I had a dream that there were ten people trespassing in the upstairs apartment in my home and that I had made them leave. Dad said it was a clearing, and a very good one.

Throughout our chats, and being aware of my obsessive personality, Dad frequently stressed, "Allow things to fall into place without your nudging them." There was an emptying of certain areas of my life, not without good reason. It was emptying to fill up more appropriately, as I learned.

In December 2009, I dreamed that I had murdered a man, dismembered his body, and thrown it in the garbage. Afterwards, I had been happy about what I had done, and so was my dad. Dad was in the background of the dream with a very happy attitude. It was about murdering the old me, so that a new and improved version of myself could take its place. The dream was quickly followed by the words: "This is the calm before the celebration."

Near Christmas, I had a dream that I had poisoned rats in my basement. Dad explained the significance of the dream, "It came to rid your life of negative thoughts and defeatist thinking." As graphic and disturbing as it was, the dream showed me another form of clearing that allowed me to fill up with something new and positive.

Another recurring topic with Dad has been that of mind over matter. In early 2010 he advised: "It is all in the mind. That means, keep your mind clear and positive. Focus on what you want and give no thought to what you do not want."

Dad often gave me good news, and when I doubted what he was communicating, he patiently expressed understanding, support, and encouragement. "Honor yourself" was often his message. "Forget about making other people happy. Focus on yourself."

During January 2010, a group of Korean magazine executives were interested in having me star in a television series they were proposing to a Korean station. They asked me to write a script that would show me taking a group of Korean children to an American supermarket and going from section to section discussing how the supermarket was designed. If the pilot caught the interest of the station, additional episodes of me taking the children to a school, a library, a police department, and a grocery store would follow. I was to be the Mr. Rogers of Korean television!

I entered this venture with my usual vigor and enthusiasm quickly delivering the first script. The magazine executives who were amazed at how well it had been devised received it with much applause.

However, through it all, I somehow felt alone in this project. This feeling was a bit surprising since, after all, the executives had approached me on this, not the other way around. Without even asking the question, Dad made me aware of the scattered energy projected by the producer and told me not to place too much of my own energy beyond what I had already done. As a result of that advice, I was prepared when the Korean magazine executives dropped the project without doing anything to sell it. Having been in touch with Spirit allowed me to be forewarned and prepared to respond accordingly.

I was invited to visit a friend in Germany. I had met this woman several years earlier while visiting Tuscany, and we had kept in touch. Dad advised me against accepting the invitation, and I followed his advice since the complexity would have been rather uncomfortable, to say the least. Yet again, Spirit was creating a win-win situation for all involved. Dad said that the two of us had a strange link, and added, "You have a connection from a previous life and are both trying to figure it out in this one. You are two very special people and are acting out a karmic necessity to learn love from one another. Be both teachers and students in this classroom of Earth."

Three women showed interest in me during that summer. Dad said, "One is afraid, one is immature, and one is complicated. Enjoy them all, but attach to none of them."

At the end of September, I received very strong indications from Rowland & Littlefield that they were interested in publishing my first book, *Thinking In English*. This came after sending fifty or so proposals to fifty different publishing companies around the country. That night, Dad affirmed, "Rowman & Littlefield is a strong beginning on your road to success." I signed with them, and my first book was successfully published the following year as Spirit had predicted months before. As all this was happening, Spirit was already encouraging me to start working on *Spirit Lives!*.

During the autumn of 2010, one of my former ESL students had been interested in purchasing a trucking company in New Jersey. He asked me for advice, and I turned to Dad that very evening for his. Dad's reply was strong and direct, "Your student is making a mistake in buying the trucking company, but it is a mistake caused by his wife."

I relayed Dad's advice to my student without mentioning his wife's influential role for fear it might cause marital disharmony between them. I simply said that all indications warned against it, and that I believed it would be ill advised to enter into a business about which neither he nor his wife knew absolutely anything. Sadly, his wife coerced him into buying the company, which failed miserably within a few months. I never learned exactly how much they lost in the deal, but I am sure it was in the hundreds of thousands of dollars.

Once again, whenever the communications had to do with relationships, Spirit always projected a win-win energy towards all parties involved. There was never the slightest feeling of partiality in Dad's advice. Spirit always holds this broad, altruistic approach to problem solving. I have never detected the intention to hurt or to challenge anyone with insurmountable obstacles. The advice was always helpful and supportive of everyone.

A humorous moment came in October 2010 as I was on the brink of having some new experiences that I felt would be good for me. When I hesitated in fear, Spirit advised, "You are comfortable with what you have and are afraid to venture into un-chartered waters. I can assure you that the un-chartered waters are better than the waters you are currently in. We will welcome and greet you in the new waters. You are so close to entering a world beyond description. Take a leap of faith and you will ask 'why haven't I done this before?'" The very next day, Dad added, "You have entered a special, magical part of your life which you will enjoy fully." There is incredible consistency to the messages from Spirit.

Dad also helps with everyday, mundane situations. In November 2010, my car's lease was about to expire. Uncertain as to what make or model to get, I inquired of him if it would be prudent to short-term lease a used car from a leasing company that specialized in such deals. The company was Condemi Motors in Lodi, New Jersey, and Dad assured me that they were "a solid short term car leasing company." On his recommendation, I went forward and successfully leased a used Civic.

Late in 2010, I was taking ballroom dancing lessons at a New York City studio. I saw them as nothing more than recreation, but Spirit pointed out that they were positively transforming my energy in ways beyond anything I could have envisioned. In taking these classes, I was opening to all the abundance about to enter my life; I was dancing in New York City!

All throughout the fall, there was much talk about the concept of forthcoming abundance, and, whenever I followed my intuition, I was solidly supported and encouraged by Spirit. Slowly, a new and sturdy philosophy of living was being constructed. Every time I followed Spirit's suggestions, I was led to situations that affirmed my connection to the divine.

Spirit oversaw every step I took. Inspirational material, newspaper articles, books, interviews, and even movies were brought to my attention as I worked on the research for the book you are now reading. It was fascinating to observe how little tidbits of information would reach me in unexpected ways. The trick was to remain ever open to seeing, hearing, and accepting them as they appeared.

Tomorrow's Children at the Hackensack University Medical Center in Hackensack, New Jersey is one of my favorite foundations. In November, they held a fund raising cocktail party and I bought two tickets to show my support. I asked my friend Nick Calabrese to attend with me and he gladly accepted.

When Nick and I entered the ballroom at the Glenpointe Marriott Hotel, we were told that the event sponsors were selling $20 tickets for a variety of gifts they were raffling. Among the possible prizes, I noticed a snazzy 26" bicycle. Nick yelled over to me, "Hey, John, here is a bicycle for you!" I yelled back, "I am going to win that bike and give it to your daughter, Ciara." Nick looked at me in disbelief and smiled. Somehow, the certainty that I would win the bike had overtaken me; I knew it would be in Ciara's hands before she went to bed that very night.

Between our arrival and 9 pm, the time of the drawing, Nick and I mingled, socialized, and treated ourselves to the plentiful amount of food available. At one point, I noticed a roving photographer taking random pictures of the event. It was around 8 pm when I politely approached him and asked if he was going to take a picture of me later on when I won the bicycle. He looked at me as though I was crazy and laughed. That was not very nice, but I silently forgave him and remained confident. I could not let any unenlightened thoughts interfere with the manifestation principles I could feel operating all around me.

The magical hour of 9 pm found me still calm and confident in the knowledge that I would win the bicycle. The 300 plus people in the ballroom had separated Nick and me from one another, and he was now near the area where the winning tickets were being announced. All of a sudden, I heard Nick yell out, "John, you won!" I calmly walked over to the other side of the ballroom holding the winning ticket in my hand. "How did you do it?" he asked incredulously. "I don't know how because the how is not up to me," I said. All I knew was that I would win. My job had only been to hold the firm belief that it would happen. The "how" was left up to Spirit.

In December 2010, I began preparing for a book presentation at the Hoboken Public Library. The president of the library's board of directors knew I was writing a book about teaching English, and invited me to present it there. *Thinking In English* was completed by then, but I had not yet signed a contract with a publishing company. Strange as it may seem, two weeks after announcing the book's forthcoming publication during the library appearance, I had a signed deal with Rowman & Littlefield. The sequence of events from affirming the publication with a public announcement to the signing of the contract was uncanny.

In the first months of 2011, Southpole reinstated their in-house ESL program and invited me back to teach it. Going back to serving my students caused me to start the year filled with gratitude.

Things continued developing at a break-neck speed for me in everything regarding the publication of my book. In January, I followed the simple straightforward editing points that Rowman & Littlefield had outlined for me. There was some minor stress due to the person editing the book. His edits were not acceptable to the publisher, and I was eventually guided by Spirit to ask him to step away from his editing duties. I met with a lot of resistance on his part, but the decision was a good one that ultimately allowed me to find a new and more suitable person to perform the edits. Following Spirit was becoming my way of life.

Dad also guided me to clear inappropriate people out of my life. He was not just referring to the editor, but there were other people from my personal life who also had to be thanked, blessed, and released. A major cleansing was in progress. At one point, Dad said, "The flower is growing, but the growth is invisible to you now."

Much of the spring was about learning to love myself, and accepting the fact that my book was going to be published. The acceptance of such abundance was a powerful and significant shift for me. The clearing work continued, and I started to develop the ability to quickly and clearly see people and recognize their true intentions. Whenever I was able to discern that a person did not have my best interest at heart, Spirit always recommended that I bless them and get on with my own life.

We have more control over our lives than we think. Many of us believe that our misfortunes are due to outside forces like astrology or bad luck, and that our good fortune is due to the opposite — pure good luck. I have learned that we have tremendous, even complete, control over our lives. As Dad put it one evening, "You are the CEO of your life." Now, this can be both frightening and liberating at the same time, but once you think about it, you will see that it is the most liberating message anyone could receive. The concept of being in control of your life suddenly makes abundance limitless and the possibilities of that abundance cosmic in nature.

During the spring, I was thinking of doing several improvements to my home; such things as attic insulation, improvements to the backyard, painting the front of the house, and a new roof. Spirit guided me through every decision I had to make to get the various projects done. These so called mundane activities were well within Spirit's domain; everything is within Spirit's domain because Spirit is energy and energy is everything. Reach out to Spirit with any concern or question on any topic.

There is nothing more essential for an emotionally and physically healthy life than self-love. The old adage "to be your own best friend" is eternally wise, and Dad could not have stressed it enough during our conversations. Self-love may often require you to stand up for yourself in the face of those trying to harm you, and even in the face of friends who may be taking you for granted. Self-love, self-respect, and self-esteem are all synonymous.

By the middle of 2011, my energy had changed sufficiently for me to become aware of the difference. For months, I had been assiduously working on clearing negative energy affecting my life, and the fruits of that work were showing in extraordinary ways. Dad said, "Things are opening up for you on all fronts."

When I began meditating and going to my father every night, I could not have imagined the volume of information that practice would produce. After three years of nightly meditations, there are seven hundred pages of accurate, invaluable advice in my hands. I began the practice as someone needing guidance from Spirit, but quickly realized that this type of meditation was a doorway to a world otherwise unknown, a world that had previously been a mystery to me. This world was eager to supply answers to all of my questions. It is an unselfish source — a wellspring of wisdom.

Ultimately, we have the answers to our questions within us. It is a matter of tapping into that place where they become accessible. If I can do it, so can you. It is time we drop the myth that meditation is only for a special few and realize that all of us could be blessed by establishing these life-changing connections to Spirit.

AKA - MY GIFT FROM SPIRIT

In February 2007, I booked a flight to Jackson Hole, Wyoming in the belief that my book, *Thinking in English*, was nearing completion. I had wanted to copy the James Caan character in the movie *Misery* by confining myself to a hideout and finish my book. Was I wrong! As it turned out, I had four more years of writing ahead of me before *Thinking in English* would go to press in January 2012, but at the time, I was certain I was soon to become a published author.

I chose Jackson Hole at the height of ski season in order to be in the middle of untamed nature far away from familiar surroundings. There are few places on Earth as breathtakingly beautiful as Jackson Hole in the middle of winter. The energy of nature fueled my creativity, and it was in this powerfully inspiring environment that I wanted to write.

Jackson Hole, a skier's paradise during February, is located in the midst of the Rocky Mountains. When my plane landed, I walked along the tarmac, mouth agape, in awe of all the beauty. I instantly knew it would be the perfect week for me since I did not ski and could use the time to complete my book. I was exactly where I was supposed to be.

I gathered my luggage and hopped in a taxi to the famous Wort Hotel where I would be staying. The Wort, located in the center of town, was the setting in and around which one of the most famous American westerns, *Shane*, was shot in 1953. I had been inspired, intuitively led, to choose this location, but little did

I know, as I rode in that taxi, of the experience that awaited me! Little could I have imagined the magic I would be a part of as soon as I entered my hotel room!

The taxi left me in front of the hotel and I quickly registered and was given the key to my room. The Wort being an older hotel without an elevator, I walked up the main staircase to the second floor. Once inside my room, I placed my luggage on the bed and turned to switch on the lights. Much to my surprise, only the bathroom light went on. I called the main desk and told them of my situation. "Don't worry, Dr. Muciaccia," the clerk said, "we'll have someone up in a few minutes."

A minute or two later, there was a knock at the door. I opened it to find a Filipino with a smiling face who introduced himself as the maintenance man and told me his name was Aka. As I explained the problem with the lights, his face lit up and his smile grew even wider, before he announced, "There is no lighting problem in this room. They sent me here to help you. They always send me to help creative people finish their projects." With those mysterious words, he gently flicked the light switch, and all the lights in the room immediately went on. I was dumbfounded.

I stood there in utter amazement. How did Aka know that I was there to finish a creative project? How did he know the electricity was working properly? Why was he so calm, smiling confidently, when he entered the room? What was I experiencing? Was this some sort of a trick at my expense? In that moment, it seemed as though room 224 had drifted into the twilight zone.

Aka told me that he was from the Philippines and part of the hotel maintenance staff, but that he had a much bigger job than maintaining the building. He said that I had been selected and that the only reason he was brought into my hotel room had been to encourage me. The electricity problem had just been an excuse to bring him into my life. He assured me that this was not a joke the hotel was playing, but that I had been chosen by Spirit to receive encouragement. He said that the book I was writing, as well as those that were to follow, were spiritually inspired and supported. After a few minutes of this conversation, I knew this was going to be "the" adventure of my life.

Aka also told me to go to Hidden Falls. He explained that it was part of the Teton National Park only a few miles from the hotel near the Yellowstone National Park. He said I had to go there and meditate because it was a power spot where Spiritual Masters gathered, and it would be extremely beneficial for me to experience its energy. He referred to it as a magical place that would prove invaluable not only in the writing of my books, but also in my life in general.

Aka and I talked for another fifteen to twenty minutes before he left. He wanted me to call him the next day on his cell phone, and it was not until I did and he answered that I convinced myself that he in fact existed and that the experience of the previous day had not been a dream.

I was not able to visit Hidden Falls during that trip, but made a point of going back the following year during the last three days of summer with the express purpose of visiting the falls. I felt I had to follow Spirit's guidance without faltering.

When I returned to Jackson Hole in September 2008, I booked a taxi ride to the entrance of the Grand Teton National Park. Once inside the park, I was told that I would have to take a short boat ride to the other side of the lake in order to get to the trail for Hidden Falls. There were not many people visiting the park at that time of the year, so besides the captain and a young married couple, I had the boat all to myself for the fifteen-minute ride.

Soon upon arriving to the other shore, the young couple parted from me. They were not going to Hidden Falls and had no interest in doing so. Initially, I had wanted company on this journey, but when I realized they were going elsewhere, I was happy to be on this adventure alone. I would have the company and the direction of Spirit.

At the end of the summer all the trails were overgrown with trees and bushes, so entering the trail was an interesting experience in and of itself. A thick growth had accumulated over the growing season making the entrance a veritable challenge.

I lost my way about ten minutes after starting on the trail. Ten minutes became thirty and I still could not see nor hear anything that resembled Hidden Falls. I had assumed that I would be able to hear the falls from a distance, but I was wrong. After forty-five minutes, I was still in the middle of overgrown flora with no idea of where to go. I could tell I was advancing up the side of a mountain, but had no real understanding of where I was. The directions the captain had given me had been obviously intended for a native of the area and not for a tenderfoot such as myself. These falls were called Hidden Falls for a reason!

I doubled my efforts to find the way, and sent out a strong message to Spirit, "I want to find Hidden Falls now!" In an instant, a Park ranger complete with green uniform and a Smokey the Bear hat materialized on the trail about thirty feet away from me. He told me that I had just passed the entrance a few feet away and to keep my eyes open for a sign on the side of the trail. I thanked him and walked back the few feet barely avoiding missing the sign again as it was mostly covered by the overgrown forest.

I was finally there. A year and a half after being told of the importance of my visit, I had finally made it. The falls were only about a hundred yards off the main trail; the sound of the water was covered by that of the wind blowing in the trees and the bushes. I was struck by the isolation of this natural beauty. About 80 feet in height and 30 feet wide, the falls gave out a low sounding roar that landed at my feet. I was standing on a small wooden bridge under which the water traveled down to the lake I had just crossed.

The instructions I had received from Aka a year and a half earlier had been to sit and meditate for about an hour — that was my mission. I sat and opened my mind to whatever good was about to enter. At one point, I heard hikers on the trail heading my way, so I quickly retreated into the nearby woods until they left and I was able to reclaim my spot on the bridge. I felt embraced by the gentle roar of the waterfalls; a sound that seemed to engulf me in love. I had the deepest conviction that I was, at that moment, exactly where I was supposed to be.

I slowly settled into a meditative state and allowed myself to be fully present. Past experiences and future expectations were of no importance to me. For perhaps the first time in my life, I was fully in the moment and joyous to be. I was one with life. I was connected to and with everything in the Universe physically, mentally, emotionally and spiritually as Spirit conveyed the message that my writing projects, no matter the topic, would be about helping and providing guidance to others — a noble assignment indeed.

I had a feeling of pure peace all throughout the meditation. My mind and body were completely at ease, and I knew I was being cared for and guided every step of the way. I had no worry about the "hows" or the "whys" of what I was doing. I knew that I was on a "guided mission" overseen by Spirit.

After concluding the mediation, I made my way down the trail to catch the boat back. I had it all to myself this time. On the other side of the lake, a taxi was waiting to bring me back to the Wort.

I had dinner in the hotel restaurant that night, still buzzing from the whole experience. I realized how fortunate I had been to go visit a place where Spiritual

Masters gathered every night and share in their special energy. After dinner, I walked outside the hotel into the unmistakable atmosphere of a brewing thunderstorm. Not wanting to miss it, I stayed and witnessed the greatest natural show of thunder and lightning I had ever seen — a fitting way to end a most magical day.

Why this was all happening to me was a mystery. Could it be that Spirit was writing the book and that I was merely a conduit for its work? Was I being used to help others? Whatever the reason, Aka's visit to my hotel room had given me immeasurable motivation and confidence. He was an unforgettable gift from Spirit.

During the following couple of years, I completed *Thinking in English* and experienced its successful publication. All along, I kept thinking of the positive imprint that meeting Aka had left on me. My life has been completely changed as a result of that meeting.

The adventure that began with a room in darkness and ended with a lightning storm had opened me up to all the good ahead of me both in the world of publishing and in my private life. Spirit's unfathomable ways are more wondrous than anything anyone can convey.

ELLIS ISLAND
ON THE "RIGHT" DAY!

Ellis Island is located in the upper bay of the Hudson River in the New York City harbor, just off the coast of New Jersey. In 1890, President Benjamin Harrison designated it as a Federal immigration station and it opened its doors in January 1892. From 1892 until 1954, when it was decommissioned after 62 years of service, Ellis Island welcomed millions of immigrants into the United States. It was the law that everyone trying to enter the country had to undergo both a medical examination and a legal interview; Ellis Island was the place where these procedures were carried out.

In 1907, 1.25 million immigrants came through Ellis Island. One of them was an eight-year old boy who would eventually become my father. Dad immigrated to the United States, along with his parents and sisters, from a small city called Trani in the southeast coast of Italy.

All my life, I heard Dad tell stories of his immigration; stories about the long trans-Atlantic voyage, the very foreign experience of landing at Ellis Island, and of entering a new school where all the kids spoke this unusual sounding language called English. He told his stories with such color that I always felt as though I had been there with him going through the adventure of coming to

America. Dad's stories had an optimistic tone, and he was ever grateful to the United States for leading him and his family to a new life full of opportunity.

Shortly after his passing in 1993, I had Dad's name inscribed on a plaque hanging in the Italian section of Ellis Island. There was a program run by Lee Iacocca, the former CEO of Chrysler Motors, and for one hundred dollars Dad's name would be there forevermore. In 2004, I decided to visit Ellis Island to see the inscribed plaque and to trace Dad's immigration using the computer center where they offered a search of your loved ones' immigration records for a fee of five dollars.

In August, I phoned Ellis Island to purchase a ferry ticket — to get to the island, it is necessary to take a short ferry ride from Liberty State Park in Jersey City, New Jersey. I gave the ticket agent my name along with my American Express card number, and told him that I was interested in a ticket for Labor Day, which that year fell on September 6. The agent proceeded with the transaction only to tell me that my card had been declined. He jokingly asked if I had paid my last American Express bill. I told him that I always paid my bills on time and could not imagine what was wrong. I hung up and immediately called American Express. I was told that there was nothing wrong with the status of my card.

About two hours later, I called the ferry number again, and, ironically, got the same ticket agent. This time, I decided to ask for a different date thinking that Ellis Island would probably be too crowded on Labor Day. The agent took my credit card information once again, and this time, the computer quickly approved my order to buy a ticket for September 19, the new date I had picked. For some unknown reason, I now had a ticket for September 19, when hours earlier the same credit card had been found invalid to purchase tickets for September 6. It puzzled me, but I thought it was probably a computer glitch and nothing more.

As September 19 dawned, I was excited about the adventure that lay ahead of me. Upon arriving on Ellis Island, I went straight to the computer center, paid my five dollars, and logged on. The Ellis Island computer system holds a data base with the complete records of all immigrants who arrived through the island.

The first step was to enter the name of the person whose records I was searching for, so I punched in *Muciaccia*, but nothing came up. The computer displayed a message that no such person had ever immigrated through Ellis Island. That was not possible! Dad could not have misinformed me about his immigration; after all, his stories were very specific in detailing his passage through the Ellis Island center. What was I to do?

I then remembered that many people misspell my name as *Mucciaccia*, with two double c's, so I punched in that spelling, and in a nanosecond my father's name lit up the screen alongside the names of his parents and sisters. WOW! I had hit the jackpot.

All the information I had wanted to know was now before me. The records were hand-written since that was the way records were kept in 1907. I looked at the top of the page I was reading and saw the date of my father's immigration — it was September 19, 1907. I asked the computer manager what that meant, and he told me that that was the precise date of my father's arrival into the United States: September 19,1907. I then asked him, "What's today's date?" He answered, "September 19th, but you knew this was your dad's anniversary date, didn't you?" I told him that I had not known, and that I had previously attempted to get admission for a date two weeks earlier, but my credit card had not been accepted. He looked at me in amazement.

Before leaving Ellis Island, I made photocopies of a picture of the *Hamburg*, the ship that had carried Dad and his family to America, and of the ship's manifest with Dad's name on it.

What had begun a month earlier as a simple research into my father's immigration had turned into a spiritual journey ending exactly on the date of the anniversary of my father's arrival to the United States. Was this a sign that Dad wanted to communicate his presence to me? Was the inability to schedule the visit on September 6 and the ease with which I scheduled it on September 19 a sign of spiritual intervention? I thought so, and felt my father's hand in all of this. I imagined Dad's spirit smiling with the knowledge that his signal had been received. He was with me and had guided me to go on his anniversary date as a way of saying "hello."

BRACO - THE SILENT GAZE

"The mind is everything. What you think you become."

Buddha

Braco, (pronounced Braht-zoh) is from Croatia and his silent gaze is known to have healing effects. People consider him a healer, although he takes no credit for what he does believing that the healing energy comes through him from God. He has also been referred to as a lightworker, a miracle man, and a vibrational healer. Through his silent gaze, he is somehow able to change the consciousness of those who come into his view. Braco channels Spirit and the physical effects some experience are attributed to the spiritual energy being projected through him. Through an almost casual stare, he is able to send healing waves to the people in the audience very much like a laser beam.

Braco works with a room full of people, sometimes as many as several hundred at a time. After a brief introduction by one of his staff members, Braco quietly walks into the auditorium, steps up on a platform, and stares at the group, slowly turning his head from side to side for six to eight minutes while gazing. All of this is done in silence; his mere gaze is enough to change the energy in those who are open to the healing.

Braco, the name means *little brother*, began his work in Europe during the mid 1990s. He is widely known there with thousands flocking to Zagreb, Croatia in order to experience this modern day healer wonder man. He does not give interviews nor does he speak during group healing sessions. He is silent throughout.

I experienced Braco's gazing sessions several times during the Autumn of 2011 when he appeared in New Jersey. The sessions were eight dollars each and lasted only a few minutes. He comes to New Jersey on a regular basis and meets his faithful in large convention centers, so that several hundred people can be gazed upon at once.

I attended approximately 15 sessions. Audience members are instructed to remove their eyeglasses so that Braco can stare directly into their eyes. They are also asked to stand still and look into his eyes as he gazes into theirs. Since the session lasts only a few minutes, the healing stare is very quick.

There are many testimonials of people who were instantly healed by Braco's gaze and others of healings that took place over the course of a few months. Once you come in touch with his energy field, the healing starts and continues over time. I felt his energy and experienced some lightheadedness as my body began to sway back and forth.

Many in the audience held up photographs of family members and loved ones, so they would also be in the line of Braco's gaze and share in the blessings of its healing energy. Many come to him with physical ailments, others have emotional conflicts caused by family stress, divorce, or any number of life's tribulations. Some even follow him around the country like groupies following a rock band.

In 2011, the organization that supports Braco's work decided to expand his influence by using Skype. People can now go online and join in the gazing sessions.

Braco's gazing skill is a means for Spirit to manifest in the physical as a healing energy. Through the silent and focused stare of a simple man from Croatia, Spirit can reach out to offer hope and healing to those in need.

JOHN OF GOD - BRAZILIAN HEALER

"I do not cure anybody. God heals, and in his infinite
goodness permits the Entities to heal and console my brothers.
I am merely an instrument in God's divine hands."

John of God

In September 2011, on a dark, rainy morning, my friend, Sue Etzi, and I ventured
out at 6 am to begin our 120-mile ride from Fort Lee, New Jersey to the Omega
Institute in Rhinebeck, New York. I had invited Sue because she is a medical
doctor and I wanted her trained eyes to observe what we were about to witness.
We had scheduled appointments to experience Brazilian healer Joao Teixeira de
Faria, more commonly known as John of God. He was conducting a three-day
healing session where he would see over a thousand people a day. I tried to keep
my expectations in check, even though I was aware of John of God's international reputation for having healed millions during his forty-year career.

When we reached the Omega Institute, we saw hundreds of people dressed
in white exiting their cars and making their way to the registration office. Sue
and I, also in white, quickly joined them. The white clothing requirement is in
place to make it easier for John of God to perceive our energy.

Over nine hundred people were in attendance, and their energy was palpable. Looking at these spiritual pilgrims seeking a miracle, one could feel their suffering mixed with hope and their desire to be healed — it overwhelmed their energy fields. Many were seriously ill, using crutches, wheelchairs, and canes to maneuver around the Institute. Some seemed almost comatose. Others were being carried on gurneys by family members and loved ones. The wheelchair bound pilgrims were assembled to one side of the large revivalist style tent. The whole scenario had the feeling of a large medical clinic in an impoverished country or a war zone M.A.S.H. unit.

Soon after arriving, I began hearing the cries of a child. Not knowing the source, I was curious. After a few minutes, I discovered that they were coming from deep within the soul of a young boy who could not speak and communicated through these uncontrollable screams. The boy's parents had probably taken him to all types of physicians who administered a variety of drugs and therapies. Perhaps he had also been taken to alternative healers who prescribed herbs and acupuncture to no avail. In desperation, they now found themselves at the Omega Institute expecting a miracle that would bring their son back to normalcy. I do not know the outcome of their encounter with John of God, but I feel certain that his case represented countless others of a last resort attempt for healing.

Many of the participants were people who had already been seen by John of God, either earlier in the week or in Brazil. They were returning to continue receiving the healing energy of the Entity or the Living God. They were returning either due to a specific request by John of God or through their own intuition. Whatever their reasons or motives, everything was colored with a genuine hope in the belief that this man was the real thing and that through him they would finally achieve their much desired outcome.

John of God is quick to say that he does not heal, but that it is God who heals through him. He is a humble man who takes no credit whatsoever for the miraculous happenings that surround him, "I do not cure anybody. God heals, and in his infinite goodness permits the entities to heal and console my brothers. I am merely an instrument in God's divine hands."

This Miracle Man has no formal medical training. When in trance, he surrenders his consciousness in order to incorporate the spirits of doctors and saints who now live in Spirit. These entities survey the waiting people and perform the various operations. He works with thirty-three different spiritual beings in order to perform the healings. Among them are: Saint Ignatius Loyola, Saint Francis Xavier, Dr. Oswaldo Cruz, and Dr. Augusto de Almeida. It has been estimated that John of God has treated over fifteen million people during the past forty years.

At the Omega Institute, we were guided into a large tent that easily fit nine hundred participants. As we listened to introductory speeches and a brief orientation by John of God's staff, we could feel a strong energy field envelope the warm and unusually scented tent.

A young mother holding her baby addressed the audience. Her name was Miriana and her story touched everyone in the crowd. She said that she had been seriously ill with brain tumors, chronic fatigue, and diabetes, and could not conceive. She was ready to give up, but after going to Brazil and meeting John of God and the entities, she was healed and now held the result of that healing in her loving arms — a four month old baby boy.

After these speeches, we were asked to form a line and slowly wend our way from the tent to a smaller room where, one by one, we would pass in front of the entity and present ourselves.

As Sue and I approached, we could see John of God, a peaceful looking middle-aged man, seated in a high-backed armed chair surrounded by his staff. Once in front of him, you only had a few seconds to present yourself, stare into his eyes, and grasp his left hand, but that is all you really needed. At that moment, he shares a message with you, and an interpreter standing next to him translates it into English.

The messages Sue and I received — a total of two each, one during the morning session and one in the afternoon — were economical in length, but very much to the point, letting us know exactly what we needed to know; nothing more, nothing less. They were extraordinary statements both in their clarity and in their level of understanding.

During our first experience with John of God, the entity told Sue, "I know who you are." She walked away in amazement never having expected to hear these words from the sacred man. The staff then instructed her to go into what they called the "current room" which was located directly in front of where John of God was sitting. The current room held a group of approximately twenty-five people who had all been instructed to keep their eyes closed while sitting there. These people were being treated by the entities that work with and through John of God; they were directly in their energy and receiving their healing currents.

At one point, participants in the current room were asked to hold hands and to pray and meditate together. Sue remained there for almost an hour.

At my first pass, he told me to go into the room next to the current room to receive a spiritual blessing; a curtain separated the two rooms. I was there for about twenty minutes and received a blessing along with a dozen other people.

After the marvelous morning experiences, we went for lunch on the grounds of Omega — vegetable soup with an entrée of vegetables and beans. Our drinks were equally healthy making us wish we ate like that every day!

Throughout the day, we talked to a number of participants who were friendly and open to conversation. A man from Chicago named Dan said it was his second time meeting John of God; the first had been in Brazil. This time he had brought a friend who needed healing. We were lucky to meet him because he told us how the whole process worked and gave us the mechanics, you might say, of getting on line and what to do when in front of the entity.

Early in the afternoon, a man named Norberto was introduced as John of God's closest friend. He told the audience of the importance of loving oneself and that fears and worries are not real. He touched upon many crucial spiritual points like: enjoying good humor and sleep, eating to renew your energies, our thoughts give us life, talking about what we want, the importance of smiling, and that today is the best day of our lives. Norberto also talked about the uniqueness of John of God's Casa in Brazil. When he concluded his inspirational speech, we were asked to get on line to pass before the entity for a second time.

While we were waiting, an older woman with a cane was ahead of us having a conversation with John of God. As we got closer, we could hear the interpreter say, "you will no longer need this cane." The woman handed her cane to a staff member who walked her away while holding her arm.

This time, Sue stood in front of me as we approached John of God's chair. When she reached him, he held her hand, and said, "I'll be waiting for you to come to Brazil. I know you will have the money. Money is not an issue." To me, he said, "I am working on you."

Although we visited John of God in Rhinebeck, his center, known as the Casa, is located in Ibaniatia, Brazil, 130 km southeast of Brasilia. The Casa is built on a natural energy vortex, a few blocks wide and a kilometer deep that funnels energy to it and its inhabitants. John of God was given directions from Spirit to establish his center exactly on that spot.

It is in the Casa, in the middle of the energy vortex, that the entities regularly conduct treatment sessions and surgery. There, John of God is allowed to demonstrate his channeled energies to the fullest since it is legal for him to do so in Brazil. So many miracles have been known to happen at the Casa that they have become an almost expected occurrence by those who travel there from all over the world. Breast, abdominal, and brain tumors have been known to melt away at the hands of the entities. Impossible ailments are easily taken care of on a daily basis by the spirits that use John of God's body as their channel. However, not all who come to the Casa are healed.

By all accounts, the compound is a place where miracles happen for those who falsely believed that their lives were coming to an end. Some patients who experience healing decide to remain at the Casa for the rest of their lives dedicating themselves to helping others.

I walked away from this experience with a positive outlook and feeling energized. I was glad to have met other participants, and witnessing their struggles, I was filled with appreciation for life and an enormous sense of gratitude. Most of these people had gone through Western medical treatments to no avail. Seeing John of God inspired hope, a feeling many of them, certainly the most serious cases, had given up long ago. John of God lovingly received every case with the same calm certainty that a healing was about to happen. No one was turned away, and no one was left without the possibility to heal.

PART II

REGULAR EVERYDAY PEOPLE

Some of the names in this section have been changed to protect the identities of those who willingly shared their stories. Although all the interviewees were enthusiastic about being part of this book, a few chose to remain anonymous in order to avoid any possible scrutiny about their experiences with Spirit. The stories are true and accurate in every detail.

CATHY MCGRATH -
DEATH DOES NOT EXIST

"Death is no more than passing from one room to another.
But there's a difference for me, you know. Because in that other
room I shall be able to see."

Helen Keller

Cathy McGrath, one of the most enthusiastic personalities I have ever encountered, holds an office job by day and practices as a medium at night. From our
first handshake, I knew I was in the presence of joy. As soon as we sat down for
the interview, Cathy looked me in the eyes and said, "Death does not exist. We
are souls with a physical body and the only thing that is important is love."

Cathy continued to share her metaphysical philosophy of life, "we choose our
family, and arrival and departure times on Earth. We come here to experience
everything we need to experience and know." To Cathy, our Earth experience is
a wonderful opportunity, no matter how painful it may be. "We come to Earth
to learn, experience what we learn, and to learn the most important experience
of all which is love," she added.

Cathy feels that "we are all connected to the Divine," and that it is our responsibility to remember that fact. Even when times get tough, we are connected to a higher power that knows all and is available to support and assist us in anything we do.

Cathy's maternal grandmother was a medium who emigrated from Italy at the age of eight. She had two spirit guides and was a great influence on Cathy's spiritual awakening. Nevertheless, it wasn't until she was in her early 40's and reading books on Kabbalah that Cathy realized she was opening to Spirit.

One of her first mediumistic experiences came while she was taking a nap in her living room. She had a vision of an elegantly dressed woman with nicely styled hair. The woman was in a hospital room, with legs dangling from the bed, and a walker nearby. The woman called out, "William, where are you?" Cathy, startled, opened her eyes. She asked the lady who she was, but did not get an answer. All of a sudden, her phone rang. When Cathy picked up, a man's voice said, "Hello. This is William. May I speak to Margaret?" Cathy politely told him that no one named Margaret lived there.

Later that night, Cathy received a voice mail with the message, "Margaret, this is William. I am worried about you and want to get in touch. Please call me." Cathy dialed the number left on the message and told William about her vision. He immediately recognized the woman as his grandmother Margaret.

Cathy told him to check the hospitals, suggesting Christ Hospital in Jersey City. The next day, she came home to another voice mail from William, "I found my grandmother in Christ Hospital. Thank you." Cathy had had a powerful energy connection to both Margaret and William.

Another interesting case was that of a reading she performed for the sister of a New York City fireman who had committed suicide after the 2001 attack on the World Trade Center. His name was Gary and he quickly came through showing Cathy a dog covered with green paint. That had been a sure way for his sister to recognize him because when they were young, Gary, as a joke, had painted their dog's ears green. Cathy says that, "We all come from the same source." It is her belief that ego disturbs everything and that we must allow things to happen. Cathy uses the following prayer to enter Spiritual space: "God I need your help. I don't know what to do. I am turning this over to you." Among many other things, she credits this prayer with helping her find work. She tailored it to meet her precise expectations, and two weeks later, she had the job exactly the way she had envisioned it.

Cathy also has the gift of automatic writing. Once, her boss asked her to cover an event. She worked for a newspaper at the time, but was not a reporter and her duties did not entail writing of any kind. She made it clear to him that she was not a writer, and had never had any training in journalism. At his insistence, she covered the event, but then let the article write itself by means of automatic writing. She relaxed her hands and let Spirit do the work. To say the article was well received would be an understatement with her boss declaring her a "natural born writer."

During readings, Cathy sometimes produces symbols in addition to words with her automatic writing. To her, this is Spirit's way of communicating with and sending messages to those of us on the physical side of life.

CHRIS AND JOHN -
A GREAT WORKING RELATIONSHIP

"We are only temporary custodians of the particles which made us."

Stephen Hawking

Chris is a thoughtful, quiet man who practices bodywork therapy in partnership with his brother John who passed away fifteen years ago as a result of an industrial accident.

In December 1997, John was working as a welder in a shipyard when, quite suddenly, a support holding up a ship in the dry dock slipped killing John instantly.

Chris was emotionally devastated at losing his older brother who had also been, in many ways, his mentor in life. Although five years apart in age, they had always been very close; in fact, they had even shared an apartment for a few years. The suddenness of John's death left Chris in shock. It took him over a year of deep sadness and meditation before he could start to slowly emerge from his mourning.

Through this period of grieving, Chris received a very unexpected gift — the realization that his brother's spirit was still very much with him and ready to assist him in his bodywork therapy. Chris eagerly accepted John's assistance in helping his clients. Their working partnership took a very simple and direct form; as is often the case with Spirit in order to economically perform miracles. As a rule, hours before a client even arrives at his office, Chris has already received from John a clear indication of what disorder the client is exhibiting and a suggestion of the most beneficial remedy in order to bring about a healing. Sometimes these take on a direction that Chris could never have imagined by himself.

During sessions, Chris often senses John's presence at the foot of his massage table gently directing and intuitively inspiring him. It only took Chris a very short period of time to establish a successful working relationship with John's spirit, and as a result of this partnership, Chris's work has been enriched beyond anything he could have anticipated.

But, in spite of this spiritual gift, Chris was not completely fulfilled in life. He was experiencing a huge void of a romantic nature. During his twenties and thirties, he had dated several women only to find that none of them "clicked." Then, one day, he received a call from a friend who knew a woman who was interested in dating, and being without a steady girlfriend, he accepted the offer to go on a blind date with her.

When Chris met Carol they were both immediately taken with each other. It was love at first sight; an instant recognition that led to an engagement and a happy marriage. But the story gets even more incredible when you realize that John had had a tattoo of a wolf on his left shoulder and Carol's maiden name is "Wolfe."

JOAN BOHAN - AUNT KATHLEEN, THE NUN

"Make friends with the angels, who though invisible are always with you. Often invoke them, constantly praise them, and make good use of their help and assistance in all your temporal and spiritual affairs."

Saint Francis de Sales

Joan Bohan leads a busy life juggling the care of her active children with her part time work as a registered nurse in a New Jersey public school. In the midst of all this, she found the time to share her memories of her Aunt Kathleen, her father's younger sister.

Kathleen Connell became Sister Mary Kathleen at the tender age of 16 while still living in Ireland. She took her vows in a small church outside of Dublin becoming one of the Sisters of Saint Joseph of Peace, and held a variety of positions there before being transferred to the United States. After many years as a nun, she became the Mother Superior of a convent in New Jersey. Sister Kathleen was known as a woman of few words, but powerful in both her devotion to God and her love of the Notre Dame University Fighting Irish football team.

All throughout her life, Sister Kathleen favored Joan. She had several nieces and nephews, but Joan was always number one. Sister Kathleen had been instrumental in saving her life by finding the proper doctors and facilities to treat a rare, life threatening illness that had afflicted Joan as a child.

Sister Kathleen passed away in 1996. Not long after her death, a volunteer who looked and walked strikingly like her began working in Joan's unit at the medical center. At first, Joan believed that her eyes were playing tricks on her, but after some time she became convinced that this woman was her aunt's "clone" meant to remind her that Sister Kathleen's spirit was still with her.

When she and her husband were unable to conceive, Joan prayed to the spirit of her beloved aunt, and when they were blessed with twin boys, credit immediately went to Sister Kathleen's intersession. Joan firmly believes that Kathleen blesses her, watches over her, and keeps her company. Death had no power to change her life-long relationship to her aunt, and so, it continues.

JIM ANTONUCCI -
THE HEALERS OF THE PHILIPPINES

"Intuition is a spiritual faculty and does not explain, but simply points the way."

Florence Scovel Shinn

I met Jim Antonucci, an ophthalmological specialist, while he was taking pictures of my retinas. During the procedure, he asked about my profession, and when I mentioned that I was writing a book about our connections to our loved ones in Spirit, Jim's eyes lit up. After some conversation on the subject, he told me about an experience he had had in 1989 while visiting the Philippines.

Jim's life dream had always been to become a professional photojournalist, and he had the idea of going to the Philippines to create a photographic portrayal of the many spiritual healers who lived and worked there. He settled in Angelese City, a 45-minute bus ride from Manila, the Philippine's capital, and embarked in what, to him, would be the experience of a lifetime.

Faith healing is deeply rooted in the culture of the Philippines with some folk remedies and rituals pre-dating the Spanish colonization of the islands. These healing practices are not intended as a substitute or competition to medicine, but are ritualistic in nature and tied to the participants' religious beliefs.

Jim's goal was to capture the rituals without questioning their validity. He aimed at remaining an impartial witness; photography not analysis.

Prior to the actual healing sessions, prayers are offered in front of a statue of the Santo Niño (the Blessed Child). The faith healers held to the original concept of "one spirit" that dictates the methods used to cure the patients. Twenty percent of the people received cures through psychic surgery, and the remaining eighty percent through energy body manipulation.

People seeking help ranged from the poor who could not afford conventional medicine to the affluent who had been declared beyond help by Western medicine. Foreigners whose doctors had given up on them were also patiently waiting their turn.

The healers tended to the superstitious and the skeptical alike, but reminded all of the essential role faith plays in the healing process. Belief is at the core of the work, and participants were asked to pray along with the healers. For Jim, and those who have seen his photos, the work is absolutely miraculous.

One day, while experiencing the local cockfights, Jim met a man who offered to introduce him to the premiere faith healer of the area, a woman by the name of Lucia Laxamana. Lucia quickly became Jim's favorite healer. She was caring, gracious, charismatic, friendly, and very funny. Since she spoke enough English to carry on a conversation, he was able to talk to her for some time.

Lucia lived in a poor, run-down barrio where, through prayer rituals and energy manipulations, she served the indigent of the surrounding areas. They arrived in large groups, said prayers, and patiently waited to be treated. While most complained of health problems, some would come seeking counseling and advice regarding life situations.

While visiting Lucia, Jim was able to observe her working on many different cases. One day, she used her hands to help heal a sickly infant, on another, she dealt with a woman's emotional illness who, according to her family, had been taken to several conventional clinics to no avail — Lucia was her last resort.

Jim photographed everything he observed, and his photographs are as dramatic as the cases they bare witness to. One can perceive the profound respect Lucia had for human suffering, and although he does not have any physical evidence to the fact, Jim believes actual healings were taking place under her care.

Jim was also allowed to witness and document spiritual treatments performed by a faith healer named Gary Magno. Gary was in his mid-forties, married to an American, and had his spiritual clinic in a modern facility in the

Metro Manila area. His preferred method of treatment was psychic surgery. People arrived to a large waiting room, offered prayers, and then entered a private room to see Gary. With the aid of his assistants, he performed diagnostic tests before asking the patients to lie down for the surgical procedures that he carried out with the sole use of his hands. The surgeries lasted five to ten minutes, and afterwards, the patients were washed and left the clinic unscarred. About a third came from Western countries.

The third healer Jim photographed was known as Brother Laurence. In his mid-sixties at the time, Brother Laurence's practice was located five or six hours outside of Manila in a mountainous town known as Baquio — the capital of faith healing. Brother Laurence was a quiet, unassuming man, and whereas Lucia Laxamana was well known, Brother Laurence's fame was limited to his neighborhood and surrounding areas. Once again, Jim photographed miracles in the making as Brother Laurence healed those who came seeking relief from their afflictions.

Jim had been led there by a woman from Switzerland who was seeking treatment for cancer and was kind enough to allow him to witness her healing sessions. The treatments took place in a tiny office equipped with a small table that resembled those used by chiropractors. Brother Laurence began with a prayer, and then proceeded to practice some physical manipulation and laying on of hands. He was a hybrid healer, which meant that he used both spiritual and physical modalities in his work.

These healings are dramatic examples of what faith in Spirit can accomplish. Through Spirit, these people were able to succeed in performing astonishing feats. Their absolute faith in God and in the power of Spirit was the centerpiece of their lives.

Jim was in the Philippines for approximately three months and his photographs have been exhibited in New York City, in San Francisco, and in Washington, D.C.

DR. JOE DEL GIODICE -
EMMA'S GLOWING FLOWERS

"You were born with wings, why prefer to crawl through life?"
Rumi

Emma passed away in the spring of 2011 at the age of ninety-five after a staunchly independent life. She and her husband were German immigrants who came to Hoboken, New Jersey in 1943, settling as tenants in the house they would eventually buy. They lived and raised their two children in that house. After her husband passed away, Emma had decided to remain in the house by herself in the company of her happy memories.

Following Emma's wishes, her remains were cremated the day after her death. Since there were no funeral services, the neighbors, wanting to pay homage to Emma's memory, began leaving bouquets of flowers on the stoop of the now empty brownstone that had been home to Emma and her family for over sixty years.

One of her neighbors was Dr. Joe Del Giodice. Dr. Joe knew Emma for the last ten years of her life and would often chat with her when they met on the block and on occasion would walk with her as she went about her daily errands. His flower bouquet was among several left on Emma's stoop.

Moved by the neighbors' actions, Dr. Joe decided to take a photograph of the bouquets to document the public display of love for this marvelous woman. As a matter of fact, he ended up taking two pictures on two consecutive evenings. While reviewing them, he was amazed to notice a bright glow around the flowers. His only explanation to clarify this phenomenon was that it was the light of Emma's spirit rejoicing in the gift of flowers!

HOWARD ROSS - SECOND LIFE

"The spiritual path — is simply the journey of living our lives.
Everyone is on a spiritual path; most people just don't know it."
Marianne Williamson

Howard Ross has always sensed that there was more to life than just this earth.
He feels that we live on a tiny planet in a vast, complex Universe, and that God is
bigger than anything we can imagine — "We are a speck of dust in the enormous
place we call space."

As a boy, Howard was fascinated by movies like *Star Trek* and *Star Wars* and
their fantastical views of reality. A few years later, by the time he turned twenty-
one, Howard got interested in the *Second Life* phenomenon.

Second Life is a virtual reality world that exists on the Internet where people
can design new lives for themselves. In *Second Life,* you can use your imagination
to re-create anything and make it the way you want it; from the car you drive
and the house you live in to vacations you want to take. No wishes go unfulfilled
in the world of *Second Life*.

Howard considers *Second Life* a way to "inspire people who have allowed
this world to get to them," people frustrated by the challenges and obstacles
that block them in this world. Earthly lacks do not exist in *Second Life*. Those
who have incarnated in lack or in physical imperfection can venture, through

their computers, into a world where everything is perfect. In *Second Life*, the only limitations are those of your own imagination.

Second Life participants can purchase virtual real estate for a few dollars, their cars can be the latest and most expensive models, and their homes can literally be the homes of their dreams. From an emotional point of view, all unreached or unreachable goals are easily attained. It gives people hope for a life beyond their earthly existence; a life that offers much more than their current experiences. Physically handicapped people, for example, can enjoy lives without impediments of any kind.

Second Life was developed by Linden Lab in 2003 and currently has over one million active users, known as residents, who interact with one another through designed personas or avatars. They can explore the grid of *Second Life*, meet other residents, socialize, participate in individual and group activities, and acquire and trade virtual property. They can also offer and accept services.

Second Life closely resembles a man-made spiritual life and its effects. Participants create the world they wish to experience much in the same way we do in real life through the energy and power of Spirit. *Second Life* is a response to our yearning for fulfillment. It is easy to understand why it has attracted over one million active participants in little less than ten years. People cannot wait to experience the feeling of having reached a much-wanted destination, a feeling that in actual reality can only be achieved through a lasting contact with Spirit and our spirit selves.

KIMMARIE ULLRICH-FLORES -
I SAW MY FATHER AFTER HIS DEATH

"Can it be . . . that you are my forever love and you are watching
over me from up above?"
                    Josh Groban from the song "To Where You Are."

Kimmarie Ullrich-Flores is an entrepreneur who turns everything she touches
into gold. A very stylish woman, a quick thinker, and an excellent negotiator in
deal making, she enjoys a considerable amount of success in the various retail
and real estate businesses she runs.

All her life, Kim and her father enjoyed a wonderful relationship. Although
there were other siblings in the family, Kim was the apple of her father's eye.
His passing in 1978 was especially hard on Kim as she mourned the end of the
father-daughter relationship she had thrived on for so many years.

In 2000, Kim decided to move to Riviera Beach, Florida, but in spite of the
beauty of her new surroundings, she was having a difficult time settling into her
new accommodations. Outwardly, it was sunny Florida, but inwardly she was
experiencing a cloudy, stormy world. She was emotionally lost and looking for
direction.

Sitting by the pool, she wondered what she was doing there and why she had moved 1200 miles from home. Had she made a huge mistake? In the midst of her emotional turmoil, something made her look up, and there, standing on top of a veranda, was the unmistakable figure of her father. He was leaning on a balcony only 20 feet away. Kim did a double take, but there was no denying that it was in fact her father standing there.

With Kim still awestruck, he smiled, turned around, and disappeared. It was a reassuring smile that spoke to her, as if he had been saying, "It's O.K. don't worry, you made the right decision leaving home and moving to Florida." It was the loving answer to her prayer.

Some years prior to this experience, Kim had had a cancer scare. She had broken her ankle in a freak accident, and was at the hospital when her physician decided to take advantage of the fact that she was already there to order a mammogram. Once it was done, she could go home.

Kim was sitting at home, waiting for her test results, when she saw the curtains move. This stunned her because the windows were all closed. Then, she heard a soft female voice speak these words: "Don't worry Kim, it's going to be O.K." Kim felt it was the voice of her guardian angel reassuring her. The next day, Kim returned to her doctor's office to hear her doctor say, "Everything is O.K." What had been in the future tense the day before had just become her present experience.

Kim also has the ability to see approaching death in people's auras. She saw her father's death one year before his passing. She perceives that in people close to dying the aura becomes "an ugly green in the center and a dull looking yellow around the outer rim".

She foresaw the deaths of a cousin and of two aunts. She attempted to intervene in order to prevent that from happening, but was not successful. When she rushed to help her cousin, he denied having any problem, but died shortly thereafter from a drug overdose. The experience left Kim with a feeling of dread at knowing that she would not be able to do anything about her visions.

Kim's gift had been predicted in a psychic reading some thirty years earlier. The psychic had seen her opening up to Spirit and being able to see auras. She told her that in the future she would be of assistance to people who needed help in seeking medical remedies for their ailments. At the time, Kim thought the whole idea ridiculous, but years later she realized that it had come true.

In her twenties, Kim was not ready to accept that she possessed a gift of such magnitude, but as she grew older, she was able to embrace it fully. In doing so, Kim realized that her loving relationship with her father had never been broken, because love is a connection that never leaves us no matter how many Earth years have intervened. Appearing on that veranda was her father's way of sending a message of support to his troubled daughter. It was the unbroken chain of love that exists for all of us with those who are and were in our lives. It is eternal.

LUISA RODRIGUEZ - ENCOUNTERS WITH SPIRITS

"You are here to enable the divine purpose of the universe to unfold. That is how important you are."

Eckhart Tolle

Luisa Rodriguez is quiet, petite, works at a bank in New Jersey, and lives with her daughter and grandson. When I met her, she had been living in the United States for 40 years, but her first experience with Spirit had taken place in Honduras when she was a little girl.

As a girl of six, Luisa was very close to her cousin Pietro who was about the same age. Every time Luisa was with Pietro something of a spiritual nature would occur. The first time was while the two were playing hide & seek at Pietro's house. As they played in the living room, they saw a bright white light the size of a soccer ball. They looked at each other and ran outside in fear. Luisa was convinced, even at that young age, that the bright white apparition was a spirit in the form of a ball of energy. Looking back, she believes she had many more experiences, but has repressed them out of fear.

When Luisa was in the fourth grade, her mother sent her to the store to buy lard for cooking. As she was walking to the store with Pietro, they began to play by throwing stones along the way. All of a sudden, two strange ladies with long, black hair who seemed like sisters appeared to them. Luisa heard them call out in a clear voice, "Muchachos!" and clap their hands. She felt they were good spirits protecting them.

Some years later, when Luisa was seventeen, Pietro was walking her back home, and as they walked, Luisa saw an apparition that she compares to Casper the friendly ghost. It was flying down the outside staircase of her house and into the forest. It flew slowly enough for her to clearly identify it as a ghost.

As an adult, Luisa continues to experience unusual occurrences. In 2001, she heard the sounds of pots and pans being struck in her home when there was no one present to make the sounds. And, again, in 2003, Luisa was having lunch in the basement of the bank where she worked when she saw a lady who went into the restroom and never came out; the woman utterly vanished. Even more recently, she had a friend, a hairstylist, come back to say good-bye soon after her death.

Luisa also believes that she had contact with an alien from another dimension. He appeared as a very well dressed man with shiny shoes, perfect in all ways. The alien approached her, looked deep into her eyes, but never said a word.

Luisa remains open to Spirit and, therefore, Spirit continues to present itself to her.

MARIE STINSON -
THE SNAPPING CLOTHESPINS

"Only a life lived for others is a life worthwhile."

Albert Einstein

When Marie Stinson's mother, Josephine "Josie" Giangolano, passed away during the Christmas holidays in 1993, Marie thought she would lose her sanity. Somehow, in her mind, her mother would live forever and stay with her all her life, even though that thought was impossible in the face of reality.

One day, soon after Josie's death, Marie was sitting in her backyard when the reality of her mother's death hit her. She began to pray, asking for guidance on how to survive without her mother in her life. All of a sudden, the clothespins on the backyard line began snapping off. It was a calm, sunny day, and there were no clothes hanging on the line. Marie instantly knew it was an answer to her prayers. Her mother had heard her and was responding in a most unusual way. Marie got her mother's message, "I am with you now and all the time watching over you and the children."

About the same time, Marie had a very meaningful dream. She was on the ground floor of her house and her mother was asleep on the top floor. All of a sudden, the house next door caught on fire. Marie, concerned with her mother's safety, ran upstairs to see if she was all right. As she went into her mother's room, she saw her mother and heard her say, "Marie, do not worry. I am fine." That dream, along with the clothespins snapping, relieved Marie of the concern she had for her mother's spirit.

Marie has since sensed her mother's involvement during many other difficult times in her life. When one of her daughters was experiencing a particularly difficult delivery, and the medical team cleared the room, Marie turned to her mother in prayer. All at once, the obstetrician came with the news that things had turned around and both her daughter and grandchild were doing fine. Marie attributes that turnaround to her mother's intervention.

Another of Marie's daughters, Erin, was away attending school when her college dormitory caught on fire on the night of January 19, 2000. This was the infamous Seton Hall University Boland Hall fire in South Orange, New Jersey; a fire that caused the deaths of three students and injuries to countless others.

As Erin exited her dorm room, she turned to the right in order to leave Boland Hall, but an amber colored glow told her it was dangerous to go in that direction. Erin then turned back and exited the building from the left side, and in doing so saved her life. Marie believed the decision to go in a completely different direction was inspired by Spirit. It was her mother's way of saving Erin's life.

Erin later consulted a psychic who told her, "Your grandmother felt that your father would have never survived the news had you died in that fire, and your mother would have then lost both a daughter and her husband." Spirit works in mysterious ways to guide us.

Marie's other daughter, Stacy, got married three years after her grandmother's passing. As Stacy stood on the altar taking her vows, the right sleeve of her wedding gown kept on falling off her shoulder. This became a funny topic of conversation at the reception, but no one really thought much about it. Some months after the wedding, Stacy went for a reading with a world-renowned medium, and was told, "Your grandmother wanted you to know she was pulling on the right shoulder sleeve of your wedding gown."

Nowadays, the presence of Josie Giangolano's spirit in her daughter's life is a certainty. Marie Stinson is convinced that we live on after we die to the physical world. It took the snapping clothespins, the smooth delivery of her grandchild, the mysterious amber colored life-saving glow in the Seton Hall fire, and the sleeve of her daughter's wedding gown to show Marie the miraculous workings of her mother's spirit. In a different manner than she did on Earth or in a different state of consciousness perhaps, but Marie knows that her mother lives on.

MARK ROSSI - ALWAYS POSITIVE

"I am one with the Power that created me."

Louise L. Hay

When he was a five-year old boy, Mark Rossi was aware of a special friend who was with him all the time, a faceless man who wore a white suit. Mark felt safe in the company of this special friend who would play with him and at times even dance around the room, much to his amusement. Little Mark believed his friend was real and that everyone had a friend like him to keep them company. Now, as a grown man, Mark has come to realize that his childhood friend was the spirit of his paternal grandfather who had passed away several years before his birth.

Mark is affable, intelligent, and very likable. His wife and three children form the center of his life, woven around his Catholic faith, and his adoration of Mother Mary and Jesus. He constantly carries a string of rosary beads that were given to him when he was a boy by a neighborhood man who regularly gifted people with rosary beads. In fact, Mark held the rosary beads during the interview for this book.

All throughout his life, Mark has had a firm belief in God and in the fact that there is something beyond this earthly world, as we know it. This belief makes him feel safe and protected, and allows him to maintain an upbeat attitude no matter how reality presents itself. His life is an example of what life can be like when it is grounded in Spirit.

Once, as a boy, Mark was riding in the car with his mother when, all of a sudden, he yelled, "Mom, turn left." He does not know why he yelled that, but he did, causing their car to avoid being smashed from behind by a speeding car. Mark has a special sensitivity and intuitive sense for what is about to happen. He hears things and acts on them.

When he was in the first grade, his special friend did not want the teacher to plug a certain clock into the electrical outlet. The teacher plugged it anyway, and much to Mark's chagrin, the clock started running backwards.

As a seventeen year old, Mark was encouraged by his grandmother to go to Medjugorje, Herzegovina to pray for his grandfather. He eagerly joined the church group planning the trip and left for Medjugorje shortly thereafter. While there, Mark felt pure love all around him. The sun took on a different look and he was able to stare into it without hurting his eyes. He felt that the sun pulsates and pops in the center. Every day, he would see two of its rays forming a cross in the sky; he was able to continue seeing this even after his return home.

The sacrament of confession was also special for him at Medjugorje. He felt the priests there had a high degree of intuition, as if they had developed a second sight. One priest in particular asked him about his brother who had passed away in infancy.

The most dramatic experience of his journey had to do with his beloved rosary beads. When he arrived in Medjugorje they were sterling silver, but when he returned home they had turned to gold.

Years later, when Mark got married, he and his wife went to Saint Lucia on their honeymoon. There, he saw images of sailors and military men piling up cannons within a military fort. It was an image of events several hundred years old; a sort of psychic time travel. He was allowed a view of how things had been in Saint Lucia hundreds of years back.

Soon after returning from their honeymoon, Mark and his wife wanted to purchase a hundred-year old house from a lady named Wilma who believed "the house would choose the owner." Much to Mark's dismay, the house chose someone else, but Mark told Wilma to keep them in mind "if things fell through on the sale, as they sometimes do." "Call me and I will buy the house," he said.

As Mark had intuited, the sale fell through and he and his wife were able to buy their dream home. Sometime after the closing, Mark had an incredible experience. He saw a "warm, bright, orange orb, the size of a softball" in the house. He then heard crying from the neighbors' house — Wilma had died earlier in the day. Mark saw Wilma's spirit walk down the stairs from the second floor to the living room. He clearly saw the side and the back of her body in the form she must have appeared as a young woman.

In his spare time from teaching social studies to fifth graders, Mark volunteers as an EMT technician. One time, he and his partner received a call, but could not locate the scene of the accident. At one point, they pulled over to try to figure out which way to go, when a man knocked on the driver's side window and said, "Hey man, you looking for the accident? Go straight and turn at the second right." The man was neatly dressed in a sweater vest, had a mustache, and the look of a 'finished' gentleman. He was Afro-American, and Mark noted that there was no breath coming out of his mouth, even though it was very cold outside.

Following the man's directions, Mark and his partner quickly found the scene of the accident and were able to successfully rescue the seriously injured woman. Several months later, Mark met the accident victim who had been told of the mystery man, and much to his amazement, she identified the man as her uncle, who had passed away three months before the accident.

In the many rescues he has participated in, Mark has a high success rate. He constantly prays while performing CPR, but quickly states, "I have nothing to do with saving those patients."

Mark has also been guided to assist several friends who were having trouble conceiving by taking them to the shrine of Saint Gerard at St. Lucy's Church in Newark, New Jersey. Saint Gerard is the patron saint of expectant mothers and through the years has helped many women conceive. All of the women Mark has presented to St. Gerard have gone on to become pregnant.

In spite of all of this goodness, Mark once was woken up in the middle of the night by a large, cold, black blob of negative energy. He knew it was an evil force of some sort — a hologram of evil. He grabbed his rosary, went to the statue of Mother Mary, and prayed, dispelling the dark energy with the light of Spirit.

Mark Rossi is one of those special individuals who appears to be a regular person leading a regular life, but once you get to know him, you quickly realize that he has allowed Spirit in, and, as a result, he has led and continues to lead a most extraordinary life.

THE PAREKH SISTERS -
HEALED BY SPIRIT

"Love one another and help others to rise to the higher levels,
simply by pouring out love. Love is infectious and the greatest
healing energy."

Sai Baba

In 1999, I was one of sixty-three participants at a weeklong spiritual conference
hosted by the Arthur Findlay College of Spiritualism in Stansted, England —
"The World's Foremost College for the Advancement of Spiritualism and Psychic
Sciences."

One of the greatest joys I received from attending that conference was meeting the Parekhs, a delightful family from Mumbai, India. The father, Narendra
Parekh, had passed away a few months earlier, and they were still hurting from
their loss. I met Narendra's widow, Hari Narsha, and their two daughters, Smruti
and Chayya. Words are inadequate to describe the gentleness and spirituality
of this family. The four of us became instant friends and remained together
throughout the conference.

Over the years, we have kept in touch through e-mail and meetings around the globe. In the autumn of 2012, we had our latest reunion on the campus of Penn State University. Chayya's son was getting ready to start his freshman year, and we thought it would be a good reason to have another get-together. Knowing that I was completing the manuscript for this book, the Parekh sisters offered me their own, personal stories of Spirit.

Chayya Parekh:

Chayya shared her experiences with the spirit of Motai, a great-uncle who had passed away before she was born. Motai had been considered a living saint and a friend of Krishna. Every August, there is a feast in India honoring his memory and the miracles he performed during his life on Earth and now in Spirit.

Chayya credits his spirit with curing her of a most painful disease. A few years ago, she suffered from calcium growths inside her mouth. Half an inch in size, they were the cause of recurrent, extreme pain and swelling. She describes how, in a dream, Motai healed the calcium deposits by opening the skin in her mouth and removing them.

I asked Chayya how she knew it was Motai who had effected the cure, and she answered without hesitation that she had prayed to Motai and knew it was him and no other entity who had come in her dreams to answer her prayers. Chayya is not alone in having this kind of experience; other family members have also felt the spirit of Motai interceding with God on their behalf.

Smruti Mirani:

Smruti began her story by saying, "We believe in miracles because we have experienced miracles. Spiritual encounters strengthen our belief in God and the super power beyond life."

Six years ago, Smruti underwent surgery to remove her gall bladder. She had been suffering from a high fever and the doctors feared that a septic infection had set in her organs.

Smruti called in the spirits of Sai Baba, Motai, and that of her loving father to help her heal. In a dream, she saw hundreds of people dressed in white robes coming to her, and surrounding her while breathing heavily. When she shared her dream with her husband, he became concerned because the color white is associated with death in India. Nevertheless, Smruti had absolute faith that she would be healed. She interpreted her dream as spirits coming to her aid and pumping healing oxygen into her. What others saw as a tragedy about to happen, Smruti perceived as a healing about to be accomplished.

Her doctors, concerned that her condition was worsening, scheduled surgery for the very next day with the thought of removing part of her liver and other organs. They were not aware of Smruti's dream.

In preparation, the routine medical tests were conducted, and much to the amazement of the surgical team, Smruti was completely free of the septic infection that was destroying her organs. In fact, that morning, the surgical team visited Smruti in her hospital room to give her the stunning news — she was healed.

As a result of this experience, Smruti's belief that one's physically departed loved ones and spirit guides are always looking after us became an even stronger foundation for her life.

RABBI MEIR BERGER -
A GRANDFATHER'S GUIDANCE

". . . and we shall all live as one."
John Lennon from the song "Imagine"

The town of Fort Lee, New Jersey rests in the shadow of the George Washington Bridge, a magnificent span of steel that connects New Jersey to Manhattan. Within the community of Fort Lee there is a sizeable Jewish population some of which is presided over by Rabbi Meir Berger, the founding director of The New Synagogue of Fort Lee on Center Avenue.

The type of respect Rabbi Berger receives from the community, Jewish and non-Jewish alike, is reserved only for people who have shown the highest level of integrity, compassion, and wisdom. It was my pleasure to befriend the Rabbi while I was renting space in the synagogue for my English classes.

Recently, over breakfast in a local restaurant, he asked me about the subject of the book I was currently writing. When I mentioned that it was about our connection to our loved ones in Spirit, he looked at me with wide opened eyes and said, "You know, John, I had a special relationship with my maternal grandfather. His name was Moshe Eisenbach, and I feel he is with me now as I talk to you."

The Rabbi went on to say that he feels his grandfather is closer to him than breath and that he always prays to him for answers to questions he may encounter in life. He believes that "we all go to Spirit when we die. Even those of us who are atheists."

One time, he was in Israel traveling on motorcycle when he heard the sound of gunfire in the distance. Even as he heard the sound, he heard his grandfather's voice saying, "It is not the end, you have a special message to give". With those silent words uttered in his ear, he continued to ride and arrived safely at his destination.

After years of enjoying his grandfather's spiritual guidance and protection, and soon after his father passed away, the Rabbi had a dream. In the dream, his grandfather said, "Now that your father died, he will take care of you." And that is exactly what happened, the grandfather "retired" from communicating with his grandson, and the Rabbi's father took over as a spiritual guide.

Although they no longer directly communicate with one another, the communion he had with his grandfather's spirit will always be dear to Rabbi Berger. It was the warm caring paternal energy that only a grandfather could offer. The Rabbi related this story with great pride and joy, for it was truly the happy story of his connection with a living Spirit.

RENEE MCMANUS - THE STERLING SILVER ROSARY BEADS

"Don't wait for miracles, your whole life is a miracle."

Albert Einstein

One day, Renee McManus found a string of sterling silver rosary beads that had belonged to her grandmother's sister. Renee's grandmother, Mary, had had an unmarried sister, Ellen, who had become a wealthy woman from her investments and from her work at JP Morgan where she was in charge of the silver department. In the 1950s, Renee's grandmother had given her sister a gift of sterling silver rosary beads with an inscription that read: "MM to EG." After both Mary and Ellen passed away, the rosary beads somehow found their way into Renee's hands.

Recently, Renee's friend, Christina, asked her if she could teach her how to pray. In a tool box, Renee found some old rosary beads made out of black wood, and, after having them cleaned, discovered that the material was not black wood at all, but unpolished sterling silver that made the beads shine brightly once properly treated. She happily lent the rosary beads to Christina along with a video on how to pray the rosary that she had picked up at a garage sale.

Through the kindness she showed Christina, Renee discovered that the sterling silver rosary beads held a special power for her! It was as though Renee, in opening her friend up to praying the rosary, had led herself to a deeper meaning of the rosary beads. Since then, whenever she is faced with a challenge, she holds the silver rosary beads and thinks of her grandmother. Her grandmother's presence immediately provides an answer, and all Renee has to do is act accordingly. The silver rosary beads have become a powerful connection to her late grandmother.

There are many instances in which this connection has come to Renee's aid. Some time back, for example, she faced a situation at her place of work in which she felt she had to stand up for herself. The problem intensified to the point that she almost lost her job. For over a year, Renee brought the rosary beads to work every single day. She credits this with helping in the resolution of the conflict and her being able to keep her job.

When asked what is in the beads, Renee quickly answers that it is the essence of her grandmother's spirit; a sense of generosity along with a calming feeling of trust. Generosity and trust were two of her grandmother's strongest attributes.

DR. DAVID DALTON -
A TRAGEDY AVERTED

"Love in its essence is spiritual fire."

Lucius Annaeus Seneca

Dr. David Dalton was a successful medical doctor, husband, and father with a thriving family practice in Manhattan. At the age of fifty, he decided to sell his practice and retire, much to the confusion of his adoring patients. A week later, he suddenly passed away from a massive heart attack. It was as though he had neatly concluded his business-life knowing that his life's work was also done.

Dr. Dalton's family and friends were, to say the least, devastated at his passing; the suddenness of it making the sense of loss even deeper. He had had such a caring, bigger than life personality that his death had come as a complete shock.

Soon after his death, Dr. Dalton began visiting his daughter, Rita. In many ways, Rita had been his favorite child and her sorrow over his death drew him to her. At first, the visits were unannounced and would take place in her dreams, but soon they became almost predictable. Over time, Rita developed the ability to will her father to come to her while in a meditative state or during sleep. The encounters with his essence were so real that she felt her father's actual presence in the room. The close, loving father-daughter relationship could not be severed by mere physical death; their bond would not end with his passing.

One night, during one of his visits, Dr. Dalton asked Rita to go check on her three-year-old daughter, Nicole. Rita told him that she was enjoying their chat and that Nicole was fast asleep and needed no checking. Dr. Dalton kept on insisting until Rita began to feel it was some kind of warning.

She got out of bed and walked down the hall to Nicole's bedroom. In doing so, she had to pass the kitchen, and discovered that it was engulfed in flames. Rita ran, grabbed her daughter from her bed, woke up her husband, and called the fire department. The firemen were able to successfully control the fire before it could spread beyond the kitchen. The family was saved through Dr. Dalton's warnings.

Spirit worked to save lives, so they could live their destinies to the fullest. Spirit knows what is going on in the next room, the next building, the next life. It knows all that is taking place and how to act in order to prevent a loss or a tragedy.

Rita was used as a conduit or medium to save not only her family, but also all the other families in her building. Energetically, love is the strongest connection we can experience, and all it took in this case was one simple act of love — a father's spirit urging his daughter to check on her sleeping child — to positively affect so many lives.

SYLVIE LECLERC-CAREY - INTUITION AND DREAMS

"Love is everywhere, and I am loving and lovable."

Louise L. Hay

Sylvie Leclerc-Carey is the mother of a three-year-old daughter and ten year-old twin boys. She was born in Canada, speaks both French and English, and is a Vidal Sassoon trained colorist.

Sylvie has always felt the power of her intuition, but as a young girl, it frightened her. Her father passed away when she was fourteen, and hours before, she had had a sense that something was wrong with him. She had been out shopping with her mother and had insisted they return home immediately. Her father died within an hour of their arrival.

When Sylvie was seventeen, she had dreams of her father for seven consecutive nights. She had always wanted a certain kind of dog and now that she finally had one, she wanted her father to see it and share in her joy, but he was dead. For the first six nights, the dreams did not make a lot of sense, but on the seventh, she dreamt that the front door bell rang and when she opened it, her father was standing there. She invited him in, and he told her that she must not be sad and that he had come to see the dog. He also told her that he would come back when Sylvie had children of her own or if she ever needed him.

The dream brought Sylvie the healing sense of closure she needed to cope with her father's passing, plus her father had seen the dog she had so wanted him to see!

PART III

PROFESSIONALS

AGOTA REPKA -
AURAS AND ANGELS

"It is love that holds everything together and it is the Everything also."

Rumi

I met Agota Repka, Agi, while sitting in the waiting room of a massage therapy center where both she and my therapist have their practices. Agi approached me and mentioned that she had seen me there over the years, but that my aura had never looked so big and bright. Because of the positive auric change, she wanted me to fully understand and appreciate what she saw. Agi is able to see people's auras and through them determine their level of health and well-being. For example, she saw that my aura was reflecting the color blue — a color compatible with someone teaching or writing a book!

Even though seeing auras comes naturally to her, Agi's passion for the subject led her to study all available material in addition to the assistance and training she receives from the Angelic realm. In her work, Agi, with the help of the angels, is able to discern valuable information just by looking at a person's aura.

Auras are energy fields that expand, contract, and change color and frequency as a result of physical and emotional influences. A person's aura is a reflection of how they perceive life. Optimism, for example, expands and brightens the aura, allowing the individual to experience life more fully. A negative attitude, on the other hand, would help contract the aura and limit perception.

The fluctuations in our auras come as natural responses to our states of being. Their hues and tones also fluctuate, and in doing so reveal our level of wellness and the state of our spiritual journeys. The brighter they appear, the higher our spiritual achievements.

Agi firmly believes that we are spiritual beings having a human experience and that our auras indicate where we are in our spiritual evolution. Our spirits determine the qualities of our auras and then project them out to the outside world. Through proper training and practices, we can develop the ability to extend or contract our auras at will.

Agi was born in Czechoslovakia to a devout Catholic family. Being raised in the Catholic faith meant that the spiritual world of angels and saints was always a part of her life. Agi moved to the United States in the year 2000, and credits her guardian angels with guiding her through the process required to become a resident of this country. Whenever a complication appeared, she would place her immigration issues in the loving hands of the angels.

Agi feels that a hierarchy of angels who will assist only when asked to do so occupies Earth. It is not possible for them to lend their assistance uninvited because that would be interfering with our free will.

When I asked her to describe an angel, her eyes lit up as she replied, "John, the angels are so beautiful that it is difficult for me to describe them. It is difficult for anyone to describe them. They are so beautiful that I do not know the proper words to use. Angels are the most beautiful beings you could imagine." She explained that angels often come through music, through the piano or other instruments. Their presence makes one happy and comfortable inside.

Agi feels a special affinity for the archangels Michael and Rafael having always felt them around her. They are part of her massage work as she transmits their energy to her clients.

Agi feels that in this world of anxiety and stress it is crucial for us to find a way to become grounded. People must sit down and balance their energies as they connect to the earth. By becoming grounded, one is able to function without being injured by stress. Another way of grounding is by being in the company of trees. Agi asks tree spirits for help; often hugging a tree just to receive its healing power — in doing so, you release blocks and charge yourself with energy that is pure.

When Agi connects with the Angelic realm, she sees colors, feels their presence, and immediately knows what to do. The angels are always ready to love, and fill you with love whenever you contact them. They want us to have spiritual knowledge and to remember to love each other and ourselves. They advise us to "listen to our hearts and not our egos, and live our lives with love." Angry people that cross our paths are people struggling with their egos. In these situations, she recommends that we "stand back and send them love from the heart; send them white light."

Agi's 12-year-old son often tells her, "Mom, you are always so much for love and peace." Agi smiles and says to him, "You are right! People must believe and trust themselves and the Universe. If you believe and trust the Universe, life will take you on a beautiful journey. Don't have fear or hold back, just trust! When you do so, life gets much easier."

BRIANNE LESLIE - B + C = A

"You are that vast thing that you see far, far off with great telescopes."

Alan Watts

Brianne Leslie's spiritual work is difficult to categorize. Some of her clients refer to her as a psychic clairvoyant, but she does not feel comfortable with this type of label, preferring instead to be known as an intuitive counselor or life coach. She even likes the term "cheerleader" to describe her services.

Brianne has been actively involved in spiritual retreats since the age of fifteen. All her life, she has been "actively seeking a channel to do good for herself and for people who come to her." For five years, she studied with Sharon Turner, the author of *Awakenings*, and has also worked with Native American medicine men and shamans. In her words: "I seek out spiritual vortexes around the world." She defines Spirit as "divine information that connects us all."

Throughout this time, Brianne always had a way of connecting with something greater than her. After having spent a great deal of time alone in the woods, she calls nature her church and declares it the best place to be. In nature, she receives information from Spirit - God -Higher Energy, and, as a result, she knows things ahead of time.

Brianne feels that the "average person does not want to hear the truth about themselves," and about the people that don't pay attention when she counsels them, she says that they will "live in the Truth when they are ready." She believes that "we are all perfect, beautiful beings here to express love," and that "love is the essence of who we are."

Asked how she feels about having this gift, she enthusiastically answers, "I am thrilled that I have this gift. I have been given an assignment to show people their own light and to remember the God of who they are." Many times people "do not feel deserving of happiness — choosing to love ourselves is very important."

There are many wounded people in the world, and she expresses the beauty she sees in them when they come to her for intuitive counseling. She recommends that we all start each day in gratitude for all we have, and in turn, that sense of gratitude will bring more abundance into our lives — "feeling gratitude stimulates everything good in us." "Nine out of ten times people are surprised when they realize their life is really pretty damn good." It is very difficult to be happy when we assume a victim mentality. To this, she simply says, "why not plant love, faith, and joy!"

Brianne's life formula for success is: B + C = A — Believing plus Conceiving equals Achieving. It is a simple, but profound way of looking at creation. When we follow B + C = A, we can create the life we so dearly desire. Creation is in our hands!

About skeptics, she says that she "honors everyone's beliefs and does not attempt to change anyone's mind. In general, people don't understand what I do. It is a question of a lack of understanding about the realm of Spirit. There is more misperception than understanding." Many times, her sessions are as informative as they are psychic in nature. She strives to educate the public and provide them with the tools necessary to benefit from the spiritual information she helps them access.

One of Brianne's clients, Matt Willey, a New York City artist, says "Brianne has a way of cutting through the peripheral noise and going straight to the core of the issue. She then offers guidance based on the core issue, and it is always clear, focused guidance, specific to what I am dealing with at the time. I sometimes refer to her as a creative clairvoyant, although she has guided me in many areas. I have found her talents to be most powerful regarding my creative endeavors. She has helped me learn to trust and also integrate my creative self into everything I do."

Bob Richter, an interior designer and television personality from New York City, is also a client of Brianne's. Bob says, "A friend gave me a session with Brianne as a gift. He knew that I was willing to talk with her, but I wouldn't have taken it upon myself to engage her services. That said, all it took was one meeting with Brianne, and I was sold. The best way to describe her is to say that she's like a great friend and mentor who has extra sensory and visionary gifts. She reveals information and gives advice based on that information. She's part therapist, part spiritual guide, and part cheerleader. The information she's given me, coupled with homework and guidance, have given me a more of a 360-degree view of my life. Because she's spiritually based, her words speak to me at a very deep level. The 'secret' to whatever success I've had and continue to have is that I work hard, listen to my gut, and surround myself with those who know more than I do in areas where I need help. Just like my accountant, lawyer, and personal trainer, Brianne provides a service that enables me to shine more brightly and step confidently onto the right path."

DAVID MEREDITH - ZEN HEAD

"Man did not weave the web of life: he is but a strand in it. Whatever he does to the web, he does to himself. All things are connected."

Chief Seattle

David Meredith is a holistic life coach and personal trainer with a healing and teaching practice in the NYC area. His wide-ranging clientele enjoys the benefits of his self-crafted signature style of bodywork.

I first saw Dave at 7:30 am outside the Whole Foods Market in Edgewater, New Jersey where he was conducting a one-on-one session in Tai Chi and Qi Gong. I was intrigued by the moves Dave and his client were performing. The smooth forms they were creating as they danced through the Tai Chi postures were something to behold; they brought to mind the most elegant ballroom dancing. A few days later, I saw them again and, following my intuition, decided to go over and introduce myself.

Dave practices and teaches yoga, meditation, Tai Chi, and Qi Gong in addition to being a licensed massage therapist and conducting a mentoring program. He teaches how to stay in the moment and stresses that the present is the most important point in our lives, "The present is the only moment that actually exists.

The past is just memories and the future is speculation. The eternal present is the only truly real experience that can be had. This 'now' is where the truest and most authentic experience of life/God/oneness is had."

Dave, known as "Zen Head" to his friends, was raised in a typical Italian-American Catholic family in New Jersey. Growing up, he felt that Catholicism was not providing adequate answers to his many questions, so he began an active search for a better solution to life's challenges. Many "cool" books later — cool because they opened a new and interesting world to him — he experienced a sense of awakening to a brand new way of thinking; a new worldview.

He tells the story: "At an early age (mid-teens), I started reading books and receiving teachings that were vastly different from that of my Roman Catholic upbringing. Through martial arts training, I was consistently exposed to principles and disciplines from the East, while also experimenting with a wide variety of New Age perspectives. As is the case with most people on similar paths, I grew to embrace what resonated with me and discarded what did not.

At one point, while experimenting with some tachyon plates, also known as purple plates, I had a mystical experience while sleeping. It was more vivid and lucid than any dream I had ever had. I was in the presence of the energy most often associated with Satan. I held before me the plate that I believed would protect me, shielding myself from the dark presence bearing down. The pressure was overtaking me and the props were not working. As I reached total exhaustion and could no longer hold back the attack, I recited the Lord's Prayer, the Our Father. At that moment, I heard a powerful, deep, penetrating voice repeating, *I am the WAY and the truth.* They were the words and the voice of Jesus Christ, shouting out from my heart. The plate crumbled in my hands as I braced for the inevitable destruction that came next. To my surprise, however, destruction didn't befall me.

The voice billowing from my heart continued to sound out and with each repetition of the phrase, the evil satanic force was pummeled back. As the voice continued, the words changed to, *I AM the power, I AM the light!* Each time, I could feel and hear the impact, like a deep and powerful punch, blasting back the evil force. With each power punch, the demon cried out in pain, until it was gone. I was safe, the evil was defeated, and the powerful energy that saved the day, came not from crystals, purple plates, crosses, or recited prayers, but rather, from the faith within me. It was mostly this experience that marked an enlightening change in my views regarding spirit."

This realization propelled Dave towards a deeper study and contemplation of Eastern thought. He started practicing yoga and martial arts, and met extraordinary teachers like Dan Millman, Alan Watts, and Bill Donohue. Zen Buddhism became his new calling. It was a seamless transition presenting no major conflicts with his Catholic background since, to him, "Jesus sounded a lot like Buddha."

Part of his realization was that there is a Oneness to all life that gets lost among the rituals presented by many of our formal religions. Dropping these rituals became important to him. You cannot have the experience of Oneness while attached to the results expected of religious ritualistic dogma. Dave illustrates this point with the old Alan Watts metaphor of the ferryboat. Organized religion is like a ferryboat and God is on the other side of the river. When you cross the river, you need to get off the boat, but the captain convinces you to stay on and go back and forth. Going back and forth is staying involved in formal religious practices while missing the experience of realizing the Divine. Watts would tell his audience to "go beyond the ritual and step off the ferry boat." Staying on the ferryboat is staying in a dogma-dominated world lacking in spiritual freedom. Dave wants you to break free from all traditions in order to realize Oneness with God. Eventually, he adds, one must even give up Zen in order to reach enlightenment, "Rituals and practices are not out of the question. They are useful tools. All too often, however, practitioners become too attached to the ego of the ritual, mistaking it for the true spiritual experience. My personal method and my suggestion to those who inquire is to embrace their chosen practice fully, but without being too dogmatic about a method that they are not open to learning other things or innovating to create new ones."

Dave conceives of the Creator as an indefinable "All." He was first exposed to this concept of "The All" in a book entitled *The Kybalion*. One cannot express the meaning of God, Buddha consciousness, or the Tao in words, but must experience it outside the realm of thought. He believes that we are all God putting "himself" in the play of life; we are both the cells making up the body of God and God in ourselves.

Dave believes that the universe, of which he is a part, is responsive and conscious, therefore, he can choose to interact with it by way of dialogue, "for the sake of having a common vocabulary with it, that dialogue can easily take on the form of any 'personal' identity I give it, and what better than that of one of the many wonderful deities. That's not to say that I don't believe in God. I just believe that the concept of God is relative to the individual. I believe that this is why so many people have spiritual visions, miraculous healings, and near death experiences that include imagery and/or dialogue with whatever religion they happen to subscribe to."

Regarding life after life, Dave explains it in two different ways: there is the traditional view of reincarnation in which we reincarnate with different identities in order to learn more lessons, and the non-traditional way, in which we become part of the collective when our physical bodies die: "Birth and death are just transitions to differing stages of one continuously flowing life. I believe that something resembling a soul actually exists and reincarnates. That soul temporarily manifests itself into individual physical forms. When the physical form dies, the ego, or identity remains for a time before reintegrating into the collective of life. Later, it re-manifests as a new form and identity.

One thing I believe firmly and absolutely is that there are no actual places called Heaven or Hell. God is like the ocean. We are waves and currents in this ocean. For a brief time, we rise from the collective and take a form. Soon after, that form drops to dissolve back into the whole. We are God that manifests itself into different forms through endless lifetimes of endless kinds, forever.

When we 'seemingly' die, we need not fear losing that which we are because our personality and those of our loved ones remain in their shapes, as long as we need them to stay that way. This is why so many people report feeling that their loved ones who have died are still with them, and there are many stories that confirm this."

Dave had a poignant spiritual experience that involved his grandparents. His grandfather passed away six years ago and his grandmother a little over a year ago. While his grandmother was still alive, Dave had a dream in which his grandfather asked him to give his grandmother a gold star. The next day, quite by chance, Dave found a box filled with gold stars while looking in a closet. What led Dave to go to that closet which he rarely entered? He believes his grandfather guided him to find the hidden box, so he could give the gold stars to his grandmother. Dave went to the nursing home where his grandmother lived and much to her joy gave her the gold stars.

ERICH HEINEMAN – SHAMANISM

"The infinite me already contains all the resources I need to navigate through life, because I'm One with Universal energy. In fact, I AM Universal energy."

Anita Moorjani

Erich Heineman is not what you would have expected to find in a shaman. With beautifully delicate tattoos all over his arms, he is an artist, a painter, and a former web designer. For the last twenty-five years, he has dedicated his life to the studies of ritual work and shamanic circles. For six of those years, he apprenticed under Oscar Miro-Quesada from the Peruvian tradition, and in the present continues his research and studies with the Four Winds Society in upstate New York.

Erich helps people suffering from a variety of ailments, both emotional and physical, through the manipulation of their energy bodies. A large part of his treatment deals with the care and maintenance of the chakra system. He explains that the first step in order to correct any systemic imbalance is to check the energy body and verify that the chakras are functioning properly; that is, rotating or moving in a clockwise direction. If they are not, Erich uses a rattle or his hands to spin open the chakras and loosen the energy. Once they are open, he cleans them out, sending the heavy energy, known as "hucha" in the native Andean languages, to Mother Earth for purification and recycling. The "hucha" or negative energies come from or are caused by our life experiences. Sometimes, he will lay a stone on a chakra and visualize the heavy energy going into that stone in order to subtract it from his client's system.

After the cleansing process is completed, he checks with a pendulum to see if the chakras were successfully cleansed and are now spinning correctly. Clearing the chakra system brings the client back to a state of health, free of stress, pain, and worry. The results are immediate, and the person often feels light after the release of all the tension and pain.

A woman once came to him feeling that she was being possessed by an entity, but Erich found intrusions in her energy body instead. Intrusions feel like crystallized, solid matter similar to needles. The most common types come from traumas held in our systems. Less common are intrusions in the form of entities — actual beings residing in someone's luminous body. In this woman's case, she was experiencing an intrusion created by the energy of her father trying to manipulate her from a distance.

Erich also shared that shamans work with both animal and ancestor spirits. Shamans must develop a strong relationship with the spirits of their ancestors since many healings come through them. When asked if he had particular spirits he works with, he responded that he did, but that they vary in number depending on the circumstances. The work he does is as old as man and has been used by many cultures as a way of accessing information and healing from Spirit.

FRANK ST. JAMES -
PSYCHIC INVESTIGATOR

"We are not human beings having a spiritual experience. We are spiritual beings having a human experience."

Pierre Teilhard de Chardin

Frank St. James is a psychic, medium, and licensed private detective in the State of New Jersey with skills in the areas of tarot, astrology, graphology, past life regression, and hypnosis. His greatest contribution, though, lies in his ability to locate the missing bodies of murder victims, sometimes even years after the murders had occurred. Local police departments regularly call him for assistance in difficult cases.

Finding the bodies of murder victims is not your common vocation. Because of his work, Frank often finds himself in thickly wooded areas and garbage dumpsites far from the reach of most humans. He has been doing this for over thirty years and is extremely proud of his psychic contributions to the many police investigations in which he has participated.

Although Frank says that he was born a psychic, his story begins when he was three years old. He clearly remembers seeing the spirit of his grandfather next to his crib — an image of him holding his chest and falling down the stairs. Soon afterwards, his mother told him "Grandpa was in heaven with God." That image, dramatic as it was for a three-year old, was only one of many he remembers as a child. Frank recalls seeing a host of people appear before him in a sort of good-bye parade past his crib. These experiences were also part of his dreamscape where he saw clear images, sensed impressions, and felt the emotions of those spirits who came before him. He later realized that he was seeing and interacting with the spirits of the dead.

In addition to seeing their energies, Frank is also able to feel the emotions of spiritual beings, and thus can feel the pain, anguish, and violence they experience through the act of murder. Because of this connection, Frank is able to provide investigators with the methods used in the murders, even before the bodies are found and autopsies are performed. Many times, he has been able to present a vivid, detailed picture of the scene and the events, re-creating the murder for the benefit of the police.

Frank uses his breath to breathe in the energy necessary to connect with the spiritual energies of these crimes. He finds breathing to be an important part of being psychic, "the more you breath deeply before you start a session, the more psychic energy comes forth."

One of Frank's cases dealt with a forty-two year-old New Jersey woman who disappeared in 2007. She had had an argument with her husband over an affair she was having and was reported missing soon thereafter. After following all possible leads and making little progress, the police called Frank for assistance.

Frank connected with the energy of the woman and the manner in which she had died. He felt her husband had beaten her to death in an obsessive fit of jealousy. Through remote viewing, Frank described her house and drew a map of the area and the murder scene. The woman's neck had been broken during the beating, and she had died shortly thereafter. Frank could see the husband dispose of his wife's body by taking it into a thickly wooded area well beyond the city limits. He had covered it with rocks and tree limbs, left it to decompose, and would periodically return to the burial site to inspect the decomposition. His guilt had gotten so severe, that he attempted to commit suicide by throwing himself in front of a truck, but his attempt did not succeed.

As in every case, Frank had started by asking if he could talk to the spirit of the victim, followed by the question, "What happened to you that day?" A strong connection quickly developed, and she answered all his questions, describing the circumstances of her murder and where she had been buried.

Frank's technique is simple; he first gets information from the victim's spirit, and then asks for details about the location of the body. He will say, "Give me a visual," and from that visual, he draws an accurate picture of the area where the body can be found.

Another case involved the mysterious disappearance of a woman in her twenties. She was separated from her husband and had decided to attend a party where drugs were abundant. She reportedly left the party with a male companion and was never seen again. Frank got involved and saw her body in a swamp near piles of sand. He could also see bridges and thought the location was somewhere near Staten Island. The woman's body had been left in a car after she overdosed. Her companion had left her in the swamp and driven away with another friend in a second car. A NYPD helicopter was called in to search for the car in a swampy section of Staten Island.

After two or three days, the car with the woman's body in it was finally located. When questioned by the police, the woman's companion responded, "I never loved her" — the typical answer a killer would offer as an excuse for a crime.

Through his continued efforts, Frank was even able to describe the party where she had taken the drugs that had cost her her life. The man had not murdered her, but had definitely contributed to her death, and as a result, was sentenced to five years in prison.

Frank has worked with several New Jersey police departments. Retired Hackensack police detective Fred Puglisi, who now owns *Quality Private Investigations,* says, "Frank St. James has a multitude of amazing talents including his psychic investigative ability. I am currently working on a case with him, and expect his input to help greatly in the solution. What he does with his psychic abilities is outside of any routine investigative procedure."

Frank has also collaborated with the Englewood Cliffs police department. Chief of Police, Michael Cioffi, remembers a cold case he had been working on since 2008. According to him, "Frank was an asset; a congenial, soft-hearted man who had great psychic knowledge. He impressed us with his ability to think outside the box on some baffling cases. On several of them, he described the circumstances to a 'T' and helped us immeasurably. Frank never charged the town for his services, but was always eager to help find the victim, and to help the surviving family members as well. We would like to have him back for other cases."

Captain Timothy Regan of the same police department referred to Frank as "very level headed and eager to help us." Captain Regan added that Frank was "honest in all his dealings on the case."

Frank's work proves once again that physical death is not the end of life, but rather the beginning of a new life in the eternal world of Spirit.

GANDHARVA SAULS - YOUR LIFE BLUEPRINT

"You are not a drop in the ocean. You are the entire ocean, in a drop."

Rumi

I first met Gandharva Sauls about a dozen years ago when he was a hatha yoga instructor in Fairlawn, New Jersey. The name Gandharva means *celestial musician*, and it fits him rather well, because in addition to sharing his spiritual gifts, he is also a professional acoustic bass player.

Gandharva has the sacred gift of knowing how to chart a person's life blueprint. This blueprint sheds light on areas such as: physical health and diet, stress management, play, desires, relationships, life purpose, career, and the spiritual tools necessary for overall balance and integration.

Through the blueprint's analysis, Gandharva is able to help his clients understand the purpose of their being in this life. Analyzing the eight main areas of a person's life leads to a deeper understanding of their life path. Every person's blueprint is unique and distinctly their own.

In January 2000, after many years of studying various theories including Ayurveda, yoga, and holistic sciences, Gandharva received an insight that allows him to pinpoint and share people's life blueprints. His *Your Life Blueprint* is a holistic system of spiritual illumination that allows people to understand and be more comfortable with themselves at a soul level.

The first blueprints Gandharva investigated were those of his deceased parents. The blueprints allowed him to make sense of the parts of their lives that had so baffled him. He was able to understand the relationship they had had with each other and with him. Their fifty-year marriage, stormy at times, made complete sense when observed through the paradigm of their life blueprints.

A *Life Blueprint* consultation is meant to be an uplifting experience. It usually brings confirmation and understanding of the deepest levels of our being. Everything Gandharva does is confidential and comfortable. The sessions may be recorded and include a booklet of the printed information.

Within the life blueprint:

- The health blueprint points out the foods, exercises, and lifestyles most conducive to wholeness.
- The desire blueprint motivates us to achieve goals without attachments.
- The dharma blueprint shows us our life's purpose and tells us how best to help the world.
- The career blueprint helps us select a suitable career that will make us happy and fulfilled.
- The creative play blueprint deals with recreation and creativity.
- The relationship blueprint is about our personal styles in order to achieve stress free relationships.
- The vital body blueprint helps us understand stress management techniques.
- The spiritual path blueprint is the path of lasting fulfillment.

The message of a life blueprint supports our unique selves. By remembering who we are, our lifetimes become more enjoyable. Gandharva reminds us that we are Spirit and that the blueprint places us in the context of who we are as incarnated spirits in the here and now. He also emphasizes that our soul or spirit continues beyond this lifetime to play endless other blueprints.

After a life blueprint session, Gandharva uses tuning forks to bring the person back into balance — being a professional musician, this is a natural aspect to his work. Gandharva's mission is to help people understand themselves, and in doing so understand that we are so much more than our blueprints.

LINDSEY SASS - STRUCK BY LIGHTNING

"Nothing in life is to be feared. It is only to be understood. Now is the time to understand more, so that we may be fearless."

Marie Curie

Lindsey Sass is a medium, clairvoyant healer, spiritual teacher, and the founder of *True You Healing* in Bloomingdale, New Jersey. Meeting Lindsey makes one wonder how someone could have developed so many skills simultaneously, but you see, Lindsey was struck by lightning and after having a near death experience came back with these gifts to share with the world.

Lindsey uses all she learned through her near death experience to help others navigate their way through life. Her fascinating story was featured in John Friedman's book, *Out of The Blue*.

Lightning struck Lindsey on July 17, 1997 at 5:20 p.m. as she and her family crossed an open field returning home from a swim meet. She was struck along with her husband, Paul, and her niece, Nicole. Lindsey describes the experience as both humbling and horrifying, and as having changed her life forever, in very positive ways. She learned that there is always a gift to be found in challenging circumstances.

In having a near death experience, Lindsey was exposed to the spiritual world, saw and spoke with her father who had passed years earlier, and, most importantly, re-evaluated her life on Earth.

What happened to Lindsey that July taught her that "life never ends, it only changes, and love never dies." She feels "such overwhelming serenity knowing that we are all being watched over," and this realization keeps her centered in peace. Her near death experience taught her about the preciousness of life. She is "never too busy anymore for the simple, wonderful little things that really matter."

During the lightning strike, Lindsey was thrown up in the air and rendered unconscious. She got hit on the right shoulder and sustained a scar across her lungs that is detectable through thermography. She remembers everything going black and feeling a sense of emptiness. She saw "many lost souls" along with a "peaceful white light that was extremely inviting." She was so comfortable in that space that she wanted to stay. Then, Lindsey heard her father's voice gently prompting her to go back to Earth, saying that her children needed her, and that it was still not her time to die.

Lindsey experienced a large presence full of unconditional love that she recognized as that of an angel, and when, all of a sudden, an energy vortex opened up, she instantly agreed to come back. She likens it to a "white energy tornado," in her solar plexus. Although Lindsey was in physical pain as a result of the lightning strike, her connection with Spirit remained strong and she felt reassured when she heard Spirit saying, "It's O.K."

As a result of this experience, Lindsey developed skills for both intuition and clairvoyance — the lightning strike had opened the nerve endings in her body. She now works as a spiritual counselor and gets messages from Spirit on how to best treat her clients. She teaches them how to feel the calm, peace, and love from their deceased loved ones.

She says, "we are not alone and our loved ones are around us all the time," and advises everyone to "go inward through meditation." For her, the gift of doing this kind of work comes from connecting people to their higher selves and to their loved ones. There is "an equanimity and a love beyond human love." There is a total sense of equanimity in the Universe.

LYNN HAMBRO - PSYCHIC HEALER

"There is no death, only a change of worlds."

Duwamish Tribe

Lynn Hambro is a gifted healer and medium who has dedicated her life to helping others. During her thirty-five year international career, she has worked on innumerable cases involving various conditions of disease. She also helps clients in the fields of business and personal relationships. Lynn lives in Boca Raton, Florida.

"We never die!" were Lynn's first words to me. They jumped out of her mouth the moment our interview began. She then added, "Our loved ones who have passed exist in a different state of consciousness. Our loved ones live after they physically die. When you move into a higher state of consciousness, how can you say that you're dead? There is no such thing as death. Experiments performed at Stanford University found a two-ounce difference between the weight of someone alive and the weight of the same person after physical death. When death occurs, a cone or cylinder shaped object can be seen leaving the body. That cone or cylinder is what we call the soul. We are light beings weighing only two ounces, and a dead body is missing this soul energy. When we leave our bodies, we go home to a place of higher understanding. You come into life and symbolically play out a 'contract' which you made before you were reincarnated."

Lynn believes that there is a symbology to every illness and that the location of a particular ailment points to its cause. One must look at the problem and determine why it has manifested where it has. It is all part of the script we are working through in our present incarnation. For example, she suffered from a back injury that required multiple surgeries to have sixteen of her vertebrae fused. The metaphysical or spiritual causes behind her condition were linked to her "carrying" too many people over many lifetimes with the result of needing her back surgically reinforced. "My back was supporting everyone who came for help over several lifetimes," she explained.

"The script you wrote can be fulfilled easily or not. It all depends on what decisions you make during your lifetime. We all have free will, and can choose to take care of this and get through it easily." Some people make their script more difficult through fighting and resisting; in doing so, they fight the solution.

Another example can be seen in the epidemic of knee conditions in the United States. According to Lynn, knee problems are here to teach us how to bend and how to walk in our lives; they speak to issues of inflexibility and lack of trust.

Lynn emphasizes the importance of hanging out with happy people. If people are not at peace within themselves, how can there be peace on Earth? There are many people on the planet who walk around unhappy with themselves and at odds with the world around them.

To the question of how to go about getting into a place of harmony and balance, she quickly replied, "By choosing it, and by sharing. It is as simple as that! There are no accidents in life. Spirit comes to us in different ways."

Lynn's first experience with Spirit was through clairvoyance — her gift for clairaudience developed in time. Later, she arrived at a point where she just had a knowing of what the correct course of action should be in a particular situation. Her communication with Spirit was direct from then on.

Lynn facilitates healing by using her hands to manipulate the energy fields of her clients' electrical bodies. She "sees" wires that she then reconnects or repositions in order to bring the system back into balance. She has had success in treating many illnesses including tumors, Crohn's disease, warts, addictions, and many types of cancers.

As a six-year-old girl growing up in Philadelphia, her mother used to bring her along on visits to the sick. Lynn would touch them, and they would later report that her touch had made them feel better.

As a young woman in 1971, Lynn experienced a serious illness that left her in a wheelchair. Her doctors believed that spinal surgery would be the only option, but she refused the surgery and instead sent a letter to David Sinclair, the author of a book on healing that told the story of a healer named Etel DeLoach. Lynn intuitively knew that Etel would be able to help her. Etel was a hands-on spiritual healer, and not only did she help Lynn achieve a full recovery, but she also trained her, and inspired her to pursue her own spiritual healing and mediumistic practice.

In her work, Lynn connects with spirit guides, angels, and other higher entities. She tunes into their frequency, but their communication is silent. She admits that she "came into the planet very psychic." To Lynn, psychic healing is an exchange of energy between the healer, the client, and the Universe. As a result of the treatment, the energy re-channels and the body begins to heal itself. A practitioner's work is to change the energy when it is in dis-ease.

She concluded by saying, "There is no right or wrong. If there is a sense of God within us, we can do anything. Even elevated souls come back to life to fine tune themselves. Take the lesson that life has given you and let go of the pain."

MICHAEL CHARNEY – JOHREI

"How is it possible that a being with such sensitive jewels as the
eyes, such enchanted musical instruments as the ears, and such
fabulous arabesque of nerves as the brain can experience itself
as anything less than a god."

Alan Watts

Michael Charney came to Johrei quite by surprise. After cutting his hand in a
household accident, a clerk at his local health store used Johrei to help him heal.
Michael was not aware of Johrei at the time, but his hand healed remarkably
fast. Intrigued by this outcome, he inquired about this unusual practice, and the
answers he received led him to a deep exploration and study of Johrei.

Johrei was founded by Mokichi Okada (1882-1955), a Japanese spiritual sci-
entist, philosopher, healer, and master artist. It is the practice of using universal energy emanating from the divine for whole body healing. Photographs of
Mokichi Okada, also known as "Meishu-sama" or enlightened spiritual healer,
adorn several walls of the Hackensack, New Jersey Johrei headquarters as a way
for members to revere their founding master.

Through the use of this universal energy, one experiences a deep sense of
relaxation and a revitalizing cleansing of the spiritual body. The word Johrei

means, "to purify the spirit" ("Joh" = to purify and "rei" = spirit). Currently, there are 3 million people using Johrei in 75 countries.

Before entering the world of Johrei, Michael was faced with the age-old basic questions of life: Why are we here? What is the purpose of life? What is man's mission? Why are there great inequities in life? Why is there suffering in the world? Michael was twenty-eight, and felt lost and confused. Many of his questions went unanswered no matter how much he searched. It was not until the clerk at the health store invited him to a gathering of Johrei practitioners that he began to discern some answers.

Through his study of Johrei, Michael learned that God has a plan into which everyone and everything fits, even suffering. Civilization has reached a point in which the material has finally caught up to Spirit, triggering the beginning of a spiritual awakening for the planet. This awakening environment provides the conditions necessary for our spirits to grow and expand until a paradise is finally established on Earth. Michael sees the expansion of truth, virtue, and beauty happening now. Our material civilization had to make endless advances before it could achieve this level.

Johrei teaches that everything happens in Spirit before it happens in the material — Spirit precedes the physical. Michael defines Spirit as "the invisible, from which all things occur first," and Johrei focuses on purifying the world through Spirit.

As to the question of suffering in the world, the view held by Johrei is that there are "clouds" of impurities and negative thoughts and deeds that humanity has created. These spiritual clouds are the cause of suffering, and when we elimi-nate them, we will have a perfect world. Everything is in a state of purification. Natural disasters, for example, are nature's way of cleansing and clearing the way for our spiritual side and our awareness to grow. To Johrei, natural disasters are just that, natural and necessary.

Johrei sees a Oneness, a connection between all souls. The purpose of Johrei is to create a paradise on Earth through the development of love and the elimi-nation of suffering. In Johrei, a trained practitioner can put up his hands and, through prayer, act as an instrument of God's light or divine spiritual radiation to eliminate the clouds accumulated on an individual's spiritual body. The work is aimed at severing negative energetic cords and releasing the negative energy they keep in place.

There are invisible spiritual cords between all of us — family, friends, co-workers, and even our ancestors. Johrei energy affects all who are connected to the person receiving the healing. The light and love that comes through in prayer eliminates the clouds and allows us to elevate our beings.

According to Johrei, we all have ties with those who have had great suffering in their lives. The ability to send love to those souls is a way of freeing them from the bonds keeping them in a lower vibration. During a Johrei session, the receiver and his ancestors are invited into the Light, which is God's love in pure form. We invite them to be elevated through the elimination of the clouds in our own lives.

The typical Johrei session lasts about 15 minutes and there is never a fee. The receiver can sit, stand, or lie down with eyes either opened or closed. The practitioner is usually two feet away as there is no physical contact at any point during the session. The practitioner first asks to be a pure, bright instrument of God's love and sets an intention for the person's happiness. He then raises his hands and starts to pray at the top of the person's body, working his way down while continuing the prayer. After he feels the front of the body is done, he proceeds to work on the back. This process releases the clouds from the spiritual body.

The practitioner should not be attached to the results, but must do the work and anticipate the physical transformation that comes as a result of the session. In Johrei, the more one gives the more one receives.

During sessions, Michael prays to his ancestors so that they may be elevated in the Spiritual World, and, in doing so, those on the Earth plane are elevated as well. Michael believes that another realm of Spirit exists, and that it is necessary for us to reincarnate in order to purify ourselves. To help with this process, practitioners pray *for* their ancestors. Michael invites his subjects to receive more and more light. Michael credits Johrei with saving his life. During sessions, his preferred prayer is, "This Light will help you. Seek it out;" a simple prayer, but one that carries a powerful intention.

MICHAEL ZAIKOWSKI - THE PRACTICAL MAGI

"Actually, we have no problems, we have opportunities for which we should give thanks."

Edgar Cayce

Michael Zaikowski, known professionally as "Michael, The Practical Magi" because he channels insights in a manner that allows his clients to incorporate them into their lives in practical ways, has been a practicing metaphysician for over twenty years. Michael is well versed in a variety of psychic methods that he employs in his sessions, among them: astrology, tarot, and communication with guardian angels, spirit guides, and loved ones in Spirit. He is clairvoyant and a teacher of sidereal astrology, tarot, and mediumship. Reiki and crystal healing also form part of the tools in his spiritual bag. Sessions with Michael are experiences where "the human meets the Divine."

Michael's mother had "the gift" and was very open with it when he was a young boy. She performed "gypsy style" fortune telling while he watched and learned from everything she did. Michael's mom was his first and strongest influence regarding the direction his life would take.

In childhood, he lived through out-of-body experiences, two extraterrestrial abductions, and various visits from UFOs. He is able to describe what these beings looked like and the kind of interactions they had with him. He refers to extraterrestrials as "greys" and says that small two and a half foot high creatures inhabit UFOs.

As a teen, during one summer when the family TV was broken, Michael spent long hours at the local library where he discovered and fell in love with astrology. After mastering this subject, he began studying the tarot, psychic work, numerology, symbology, religion, and the occult. By the time he entered college, he had also been introduced to Wicca, Taoism, and Buddhism. Throughout his college years, he wrote a monthly article on astrology for the newspaper successfully predicting some of the Gulf War's key events. Over the following years, he accepted his role as psychic advisor and healer.

Michael's philosophy is that "we all come from the stars" and that angels are energy beings who are on Earth to assist us whenever necessary. He believes that we are all connected, all part of the oneness of life. In a very humble manner he expressed that he "is not doing this work," but rather that he is merely an instrument and that all the information comes from the Angelic Realm.

He teaches that Spirit wants us to be happy and will gladly assist whenever called upon to do so in the shape of angels or in the form of relatives and loved ones who have passed away. But, the important point is that we must call for their help before they enter our lives, since for them to do otherwise would be an unwanted interference in our life experiences and a negation of our free will.

Michael's view that our lives go on after physical death, is more than a belief, it is a certainty. The presence of Spirit was palpable during our interview; it was as though he had the ability to turn his connection with the divine into a tangible energy that embraced everyone in his presence. He offers a bridge between life on Earth and its continuation in Spirit.

NICOLE MILLER - VODOU PRIESTESS

"The essential thing in Vodou is not within the ritual itself, rather in what it suggests in the mind of those who are practicing the religion."

Max Beauvoir

Before meeting Nicole Miller in the Spring of 2012, my entire concept of Haitian Vodou had been largely derived from watching *The Serpent and the Rainbow*, a 1988 film directed by horror filmmaker extraordinaire Wes Craven. That concept had been rendered completely inaccurate by the time my first meeting with Nicole was over.

Vodou (also Voodoo, Vodun or Vodoun) is Haiti's chief religion, practiced by more than 50% of Haitians and the Haitian diaspora. The terms "vodou" signifies "mysterious forces or powers that govern the world and the lives of those who reside within it, but also a range of energies." Vodou practitioners are known as vodouists or servants of the spirits. They believe in a distant creator spirit called Bondye or the good God, and in a more approachable family of spirits known as loas who are responsible for the different aspects of life.

Since vodouists are not able to access Bondye, they direct their prayers to the loas, developing relationships with them by making offerings, through the creation of personal altars in their homes, and by having ceremonies of music and dance where they prepare sacred spaces for the loas to descend and bless them with their presence. A Vodou ceremony is known as a "service to the loas." Vodou is a deep, complex, and elaborate religion with a rich tradition and relevant ritualistic life.

Haitian vodou dates back to the eighteenth century. During colonial times, African religions were suppressed and slaves were forced to practice Christianity. As a matter of fact, Roman Catholicism, European mysticism, and Freemasonry were enormously influential in the development of Vodou.

Meeting Nicole Miller immediately dispelled my vision of voodoo dolls and zombies. She is an intelligent, lovely woman who works in the finance department of a major corporation. We first met over lunch at a well-known midtown Manhattan restaurant where she eagerly answered my many questions, and shared her experiences as a Vodou mambo — the title given to priestesses in the Vodou religion; priests are known as houngans.

According to Nicole, Vodou is not just a religion, but a way of life. As participants introspect, they realize that the world, in all its aspects, is intricately connected to the spiritual order. As Jean Price Mars, a popular Haitian writer, expressed it, "Vodou is a religion because all its followers believe in spiritual entities who live in close harmony with the humans whose activities they control." Vodou is concerned with maintaining a balance between the world of spirits and the world of man.

Nicole works closely with Max Beauvoir, the *chef supreme* of the National Confederation of Hatian Vodou, and due to her position in the hierarchy of Vodou, was chosen as the focus of a chapter in the seminal study of Vodou entitled *Le Vodou en Haiti - Les Mythes Revisites" (Vodou in Haiti - The Myths Revisited).*

Vodou is a monotheistic religion that recognizes one supreme entity and sees the human being as a soul in a perishable package. It is regularly practiced alongside Catholicism without causing any dissonance whatsoever in the hearts and minds of devotees. Nicole explains, "God is too busy taking care of the whole universe, so the loas were created as intermediaries who manifest themselves when called upon." She also added that Haiti is "100% Catholic and 99% Vodou."

God is seen as the fundamental source energy where all differentiated types of energy find their origin. This source is perceived as a female entity called

Yehwe who is the Mother of the Universe and the Creatrix of all existence. The Universe is seen as consisting of two worlds: the visible and the invisible, the invisible being the largest of the two and filled with the energies of all those who have lived since the beginning of time. The two worlds harmoniously interpenetrate each other, and the spirits or energies residing in them mingle. In Vodou, the soul is immortal and possesses free will. Spirit is everywhere.

Nicole tells the story of a day when she was sitting at home and a stone came flying through a window without shattering the glass, leaving only a bullet size hole in it. It was a gift from Spirit, a stone filled with energy that accompanies her to this day. Spirit uses many different avenues to make its presence known. Another gift from Spirit came in the shape of a plane ticket. Nicole was invited to go to Haiti with Max Beauvoir and his wife for a special ceremony. When she tried to book a seat, the airline informed her that there were none available. When she told Max of her plight, he gently suggested she try again. On her third try, there was not only an available seat, but it was the seat between Max and his wife, exactly the one she had wanted!

Nicole further describes Vodou as "nothing more than a cult to life, which by definition implies a close parallel to love." According to her, "Vodou offers an orientation, a vision of life. With a strong faith in God, it prescribes a dynamic approach to man's survival, a sense of hope which resides not in a mute acceptance of his condition, but in his courage to fight for change."

A week after our Manhattan meeting, Nicole welcomed me into her home where she maintains a Vodou temple called The Temple of Yehwe. As soon as we entered, she lit a candle to a vodou spirit known as Papa Legba to ensure that our "communication would flow." I sat surrounded by hundreds of religious artifacts, paintings, ceremonial cloths, and candles specifically connected to the loas Nicole serves, and to the deceased ancestors she reveres. Everything has a reason for being, an order, and a meaning in the magically ritualistic life of Vodou.

Nicole was born and raised in Haiti and was officially initiated as a mambo twenty years ago. She said, "We do good. We want things to be right." Nicole explained that often in life things "break-down, they derail... We put things back on track." As a mambo, she has dedicated her life to helping others achieve balance. Many flock to Nicole in need of having a relationship blessed, a business deal straightened, or a health concern addressed. All of these areas are within the sphere of influence of the Vodou priesthood and its established rituals designed to physically, emotionally, and spiritually affect a situation.

An interesting rite, for example, takes place a year and a day after a funeral. When a person dies, the soul is believed to go under water for a year and a day. After that time, a ceremony is held to elevate the soul and free it to reincarnate. The time under water serves to rest and cleanse the soul in preparation for its return to life.

Vodou is not found in a doll stuck with pins meant to curse or in the use of skulls to bring about disease and death. It is instead a religion of harmony, meant to bring wisdom, health, and prosperity into people's lives. Knowing Nicole Miller and witnessing her life of service, one could not believe otherwise.

RED DUKE - THE HAVEN FOR
SPIRITUAL TRAVELERS

"Great men are they who see that spiritual is stronger than any
material force — that thoughts rule the world."

Ralph Waldo Emerson

I visited Red Duke on Labor Day, 2011. He is the founding director of *The
Haven for Spiritual Travelers* in Fort Lauderdale, Florida. Born in Jacksonville of
a Cherokee mother and a Scottish/Irish father, he grew up in Fort Myers and
learned much about the healing powers of Spirit. When he was endowed with
these energies himself, he began a long search for the meaning of life. He is a
sensitive, a mystic, and a spiritual healer.

Now in his eighties, Red has encountered and healed everything from brain
tumors and cancer to heart disease. He is always available, re-charged and re-
fueled by the call of someone asking for help. Red has learned that the Source
flows through him and that there is an infinite source of healing available for all.
He credits Spirit as the source of all healing.

Red's ability to heal manifested for the first time in 1968. He was working as
a carpenter at the Broward County Airport in south Florida when, in the midst

of a job, a wooden plank struck him between the shoulders. "The hammer in my hand leapt upwards and then fell to the ground," he said, "The nails came out of my nail belt and circled round my body." Red staggered outside and met his friend Harry, who described a white milky substance oozing from Red's solar plexus. "I saw the clothes on Harry's chest disappear, and the flesh open in front of me. I saw a hole in his chest and watched as it closed up before me," Red recounts. Things immediately returned to normal, and Harry told Red about a hernia that had been diagnosed in his esophagus. After their encounter, the hernia completely healed, vanishing without a trace.

Over the following twelve months, Red voraciously researched and learned how to channel these newfound energies. Today, he can effortlessly detect imbalances in a person's body. Nothing escapes him, not a thought, a discomfort, nor a serious illness. "It's a burden, at times, to know that someone standing in front of me is sick. I can't always approach them and say, 'here let me help you.' I have to ask permission first, and not everyone is receptive."

Sometimes during a session his face and voice change character. He says, "You'll notice the change in our voice as we go into a different vibration." He uses the plural because he feels that there are spirits that enter his body and take over the healing. He is often heard saying, "We had to go to another, or higher, dimension to access that information."

The power comes *through* him *not* from him. Red's motto is "sensitivity through simplicity." All is channeled by Spirit; very natural and positive. Nothing negative is allowed at *The Haven*.

ROGER ANSANELLI - TOGETHER WE CAN CREATE A NEW REALITY

"Every thought we think is creating our future."

Louise L. Hay

Roger Ansanelli leads workshops on sound healing, frequency work, and vibrational medicine both in Hoboken, NJ, where he has his private practice, and in New York City. He is an ordained minister and certified master practitioner and teacher of I.E.T. (Integrated Energy Therapy), Reiki, and Advanced Pendulum Work. He is also certified in Magnified Healing, Esoteric Healing, and Matrix Energetics. In addition, he is an ACE certified personal trainer and rehab specialist with over twenty years of experience. Roger attended the New England Conservatory of Music in Boston and has a degree from NYU's Tish School of the Arts.

When you are in Roger's presence, you can feel the joy and love that emanate from him. The heart of his work is in assisting people to move into the fullness of their light by clearing the emotional and energetic debris blocking their way to harmony. People go to Roger to reconnect with their inner balance — to become one with Spirit and make changes in their lives. Through the use of various modalities, Roger helps them clear the obstacles and blocks that prevent them from connecting with their true selves. These blocks may have developed through experiences in this present level of consciousness or may have been carried forward from previous levels of existence or what we call "past" lives.

In his capacity as a personal trainer and rehab specialist, Roger has an uncanny ability to determine the best course of exercise his clients need to follow in order to help heal their systems. In his healing practice, he "helps people help themselves to heal." He is quick to add, "Everyone has great ability to heal." He feels that we are on Earth to bring healing not only to ourselves, but also to the planet.

Roger receives information and knowledge from a variety of spiritual sources. This information comes in while he tunes into his client's energy fields or even while he is doing something mindless such as running on a treadmill or washing dishes. It is knowledge that has no meaning to him until it is linked to a particular person or the context of a session highlights it as pertinent or relevant.

Roger is connected to Spirit and it is Spirit that guides him in his work whether through the Angelic or Higher Realm or directly from the Creator or Source. He listens from his Light — even trees, animals, and the Earth are able to communicate their messages to him through words, feelings, and emotions. At times, messages also come from the spirit of a deceased person or from clients' spirit guides. But, no matter the source, the one common denominator in all of these experiences is love. Roger explains that the angels' main message is, "You are loved beyond measure. Even messages that could be perceived as not so nice come in from Spirit in love. Spirit wants us to know that love is all around us, everywhere we are."

Roger remembers his gifts manifesting from an early age. He could sense people's intentions including his classmates and teachers. He could read their energies physically, mentally and emotionally. He was aware of people's unspoken thoughts and would also have knowledge of things before they happened or as they were happening. For example, while playing in the backyard of the home where he grew up, he would know the precise moment his mother would get home. He is of the opinion that "if people listen and connect to their hearts, they could know all that is happening." Over the years, his abilities have grown from psychic to intuitive to mediumistic.

Roger receives information and guidance in varied forms — conclusive thoughts, words, images, and especially in healing melodies. Sometimes, he sees objects and experiences feelings that make sense to his clients, even though they often do not make sense to him at the time of reception.

Even in childhood, Roger knew what people needed to improve or completely free themselves of physical ailments. When confronted with such a situation, he turns to his Spirit guides and asks for help in seeing the person, animal, environment, or circumstance as healthy and whole. He explains that this is the way in which Jesus would look at the sick. Jesus would see all people as being whole and would pay no attention to the mistaken notion known as "disease."

While a session is in progress, a three-part informational energy system is set up between Spirit, Roger, and the client. He usually gets goose bumps and hears music playing, "I physically feel and get the emotion of the spiritual message." That is, he feels the emotional content of what is being expressed through him. For example, he can feel "the personality of the spirit and the joy of the expression." Roger believes that giving readings also nurtures him. The more readings he gives the more Spiritual nourishment he receives for which he is immensely humbled and grateful.

In sessions or during meditations, Roger often sings the word "we." He admits that it regularly comes in because "*we* are not alone." He explains, "Wherever you are, love is there. A human being is one of the highest expressions of the Creator and we don't even know it, yet." In all expressions of love, it is "we" giving us the message that Spirit is always with us. As Roger channels it, "We shall be with you always. It is always 'we' and never just 'I'."

Roger advises everyone "to have a spiritual practice of daily morning meditations in order to start the day grounded to the Earth and connected to their light. Grounding means to connect with Mother Earth so that one is balanced and not living in a reactionary way. Grounding also helps us to achieve a calm physical state, to connect to our non-physical selves, and, most importantly, to the Heart. Too many of us operate only from our brains where mistakes are frequently triggered since we are not usually calibrated to high vibrational thoughts. When you ground yourself, you come together with the Earth, with Source, and with all of life, becoming firmly rooted in the now."

Roger does not use the word aura or auric field when describing how he connects to someone's energy. Instead, he connects to "all of a client" so they can work together. In this way, he is able to take in both the physical body and the fields of information around a person.

Sometimes, Spirit will give him a list of facts with the sole intention of validating its presence. For example, one time, he was giving a spontaneous reading when Spirit told him that the man had two cars, one blue and one red. This seemingly unimportant message helped establish the client's mind in the reality of Spirit. As Roger gave the message, the client looked at him wide-eyed and smiling.

Roger also employs a scanning technique in which he passes his hand over a person's body at a distance of a few inches. By doing this, he is able to sense where there might be disharmony or disease. As he incorporates this method of detecting disharmony, Spirit shows him the appropriate strategy to bring any distressed energies back into balance.

Those who are experiencing a disease are "on a learning intensive journey. They are manifesting an experience that brings them and those around them a vast amount of information with the sole purpose of moving into love. It never means that they are doing anything wrong. They are in the intense process of incorporating new patterns of energy that will bring ultimate healing whether it manifests here in the physical world or in the world of Spirit after their physical deaths."

People come to Roger for assistance in releasing this experience of dis-ease so they may move into wholeness. Roger says that "Light equals Love" and that he wishes his clients would "live from the intelligence of Light." He explains that "Light is the Creator and the Creator is the Divine Being that encompasses everything in life. Our greatest moments are when we are connected to our Light for it is then that we love each other and find ourselves in grace. At that point, there are no grievances because they all just drop away."

Roger often quotes Albert Einstein's famous: "We cannot solve problems from the same consciousness that created them." For Roger, it illustrates the point that, "we vibrate higher when we are connected and in harmony. When we are in love no problems can exist. In that condition, you live from a different place. You are living from the intelligence of the Light that you are. People need to choose this for themselves." Roger feels that you must "love yourself first and love each other, which means *everybody.*"

Being in Roger's company is a joyous experience and he considers that "joy" a by-product of love. When asked what love really is, he answered, "Love is being present. We move into fullness, and you cannot deny love. It is difficult to hold back from sharing love." Roger tells us to "stop thinking about the past and the future. The present moment is love. Love brings grace into our lives. It makes us aware of our oneness with the Creator — an atmosphere where miracles take place."

Roger loves what he does. He "feels privileged for being able to interact with the courageous people who show up seeking his assistance." He says, "They fill my heart with song and I will sing forevermore!"

Sessions with Roger are also about clearing what obscures our Light. "It is not just what we are holding, but also the lower-vibration thoughts, feelings, and judgments we might have towards others that obscure our light," he explains, "and, at times, these obstructions make us behave from a place of fear."

Roger sees us as great orbs of light, no different from the Sun. A lower vibration towards ourselves or towards others dims or obscures that Light. The main message from the Angelic Realm in this respect is that "we are Masters of Light. To solve a problem we must see, think, live, and act from a different place. The biggest thing for us to remember is that we must live from a higher vibration – from the intelligence of light."

In his Energy-Frequency practice, he uses crystal bowls and his considerable singing abilities to lead weekly meditations. His intention is to provide a place where people can connect to their Light through the healing vibrations of sound. He says, "When you connect, you are able to fully express yourself."

Roger starts getting spiritual guidance about his meditation topics well before the meditation is due to begin. The people that show up on a given evening also inspire particular topics. Sometimes, just an hour or so before, the subject matter comes to Roger along with an image of who will show up to meditate. During the seven years he has been leading these sound meditations, no two have been the same and there has never been a meditation where someone has not expressed, "this is exactly what I needed tonight."

"The heart of our being calls in exactly what we need," Roger says, "I think Spirit, non-physical existence, needs to receive more importance. It is in the non-physical that we create everything, and where we realize the jewel that we are — this is what we need to bring forth into the world. The moment we are receptive to the non-physical, things start to move and we are more readily able to give reality to our visions. There is an abundance of love in the world — we are never lacking in anything. Life is the greatest gift, meant to be experienced and shared — lived in our light!"

ROLAND COMTOIS - LOVE IS ALL THAT MATTERS

"Hope is a gift to fuel our passion, compassion and light."
Roland Comtois

The word that best describes the work of Roland Comtois is hope. Many of those that cross his path are on the cusp of despair and he never fails to deliver an encouraging message that lessens their suffering. He is more than a medium — he is a conveyor of hope.

Roland is the author of two books (*And Then There Was Heaven* and *A Journey of Hope and Love*), an internationally known inspirational speaker appearing regularly before large groups seeking to connect with their departed loved ones, and the host of a live show on Internet radio.

His website talks about his "uncanny ability to connect with the spiritual realm" and that is exactly what he does. His first spiritual experience came at the age of ten when the spirit of his grandmother accompanied by three angels appeared in his bedroom. Even at that young age, he was aware of the Spirit world, the presence of God, and the deep sense of peace that it brings.

During high school, Roland worked as a patient-care attendant at a nursing home. This led him to pursue studies in nursing with a specialization in gerontological care — he always seemed drawn to those near death.

His mission is not to convince people of the reality of Spirit, but to have them believe in themselves. It is his firm conviction that we all share in the ability to connect with Spirit and can do so more easily than we think. Even when we are told that that kind of communication is out of our reach, looking beyond the veil is always possible. Love never dies; our loved ones are always just a breath away.

Roland likens connection to Spirit to a warm embrace; an embrace of love, God, Spirit, and energy. Once we trust ourselves, we will experience the power of our eternal connection. He encourages us to "get with the program and realize that you can do it." A medium may take you to the door of the Spirit realm, but it is your own belief that takes you through that door and into a place of unbelievable love and joy. Roland feels that our DNA is "programmed to love." No matter what experiences we go through, we must "shine our light of courage."

Roland often remembers a woman he met at a group reading in Jay, New York. She had been hiding at the back of the room by a supporting beam, but, for him, Spirit placed her in a "spotlight." Calling her out, Roland told her that her departed four-year-old daughter was safely in heaven with their family dog watching over her. The woman had also lost another child, an older son. The boy came through to assure his mother that he, like his younger sister, was at peace in Spirit. After the reading, the lady came up to him and said that after years of mourning, she could now finally breathe.

Before starting a session, Roland writes what he refers to as "purple papers." In them, he writes messages from Spirit directed to the people he is about to read. He openly admits that he has no "credentials" to do the work he does, but puts it in simple terms, "I have nothing, but I have everything."

Near the conclusion of the interview, Roland began to writhe in his chair. I did not know what was happening. Quite honestly, I thought he was having some sort of seizure, but all of a sudden, he began speaking in a voice not his own that described to a "T" the last fifteen minutes of my father's life as I had witnessed it in his hospital room twenty years earlier. I was flabbergasted at Roland's ability to allow my dad's spirit to use his body to communicate with me. Dad had come to let me know how proud he is of me and to thank me for making his transition such a smooth experience — my love had given him permission to go. Mom's spirit also came through to soothe my worries and to offer words of encouragement.

Roland believes that our loved ones in Spirit watch over us and are of service to us. He explains that "the soul lives on and the connections we have are unbroken." There is no end to life or to love in the world of spirit. The notion that our souls have no obstacles is greatly encouraging, and the only barrier is the one made out of our own false limiting beliefs.

RYAN MICHAELS - TEENAGE PSYCHIC

"What you seek is seeking you."

Rumi

In October of 2012, WABC-TV's "20/20" dedicated a whole hour to the investigation of psychically gifted people. Of those profiled, eighteen year-old Ryan Michaels fascinated me the most. You see, Ryan has been aware of his psychic gifts since he was ten. A few days after the show aired, I had the opportunity to interview Ryan. Very mature for his age, he calls himself a "psychic medium and spiritualist," but his business card lists his credits additionally as a paranormal counselor, paranormal investigator, and missing person consultant.

Ryan enjoyed a "normal" childhood growing up in Pennsylvania. He discovered his psychic abilities quite naturally when he began receiving messages from Spirit and he readily accepted the information. From the very beginning, Ryan has accepted his gift in a matter-of-fact way. He is delighted to be doing this kind of work and would like to continue doing it for the rest of his life.

Ryan is an Assembly Member of the Lily Dale congregation in northern New York State. He is certified as a spiritualist and minister and as a psychic and medium — quite an accomplishment for a young man who was thirteen at the time. Ryan has given well over 1100 readings in the past two years. The more readings he gives, the deeper he is able to get into the spiritual world. He regards himself as an interpreter of the messages Spirit gives him.

Ryan receives his information mainly from a spirit guide and from the spirits of his clients' deceased family members who come back to offer their help. He taps into these sources through meditation and he finds that the more he meditates, the less time he needs to receive answers to his queries. The information comes in almost immediately. He gets the "vibration" (which he pronounced *"viberation"*) of the spirit's energy and that sets the tone for the specific reading. His entire body feels the presence of Spirit. He explains that each and every spirit has an identifiable vibration, and it is this, in the shape of a touch or a quality of voice, that allows Ryan to identify a particular spirit as he reads for a client.

When Ryan was ten, he was featured on A&E's *Psychic Kids* for the last four seasons of the show that also aired on the Biography Channel. By the time he was thirteen, he began giving readings to his friends. He asked them if they wanted to know what deceased relatives had to say to them, and when they said "yes," he proceeded to deliver the many messages. His friends accepted and supported his gift, and by sixteen, he had advanced to full fledged mediumship.

According to Ryan, the movie *Hereafter* is an accurate depiction of the Spirit world and what it is like to tap into it. While discussing the movie, he explained the difference between a psychic and a medium. A psychic does not know the origin of his information, while a medium knows the information is coming from the identifiable spirit of a deceased person.

Ryan maintains a friendly relationship to Spirit. In talking to him, it seems as though he simply meditates to connect to his friends who are without physical bodies. He feels it is that simple. He practices daily because he does so many readings, and this has expanded his life in many wondrous ways. Ryan is in contact with the wide world of Spirit 24/7, at will. Occasionally, he meets skeptics and he does his best to show them that Spirit is not a mystery, but a natural part of life. He believes that Spirit presents itself to help make our lives smoother. More than anything, he would like all to know that Spirit makes itself accessible in order to guide us and lend us assistance in our lives.

SANDRA REDMAN – CLAIRVOYANT

"We are here to awaken from our illusion of separateness."

Thich Nhat Hanh

Sandra Redman is a jolly, British clairvoyant and psychic born and raised in London. She currently resides in mid-town Manhattan where, full of optimism, she is dedicated to helping people through all types of life problems. She has been doing this work for over fifty-five years.

Sandra came to New York in the 1960s when she was twenty-five. Her first job was at the 1964 World's Fair, followed by a stint as a sixteen-wheel oil truck driver on long distant hauls, a job about which she boasts openly! Soon after, she worked as a stewardess for a charter airline company that flew American troops to and from Vietnam during the war.

During this time, Sandra met and married a Marine officer named Hugh; the marriage would end in divorce ten years later. Hugh has since passed away and now visits Sandra regularly, moving small flags in her apartment to make his presence known. Her mother who died twelve years ago also regularly visits Sandra. As a matter of fact, as I was interviewing Sandra, her mother walked through the room, and gave her approval, "I like everything about John." A fascinating review from the Spirit world!

As a child, Sandra loved to read ghost stories, and, as a teenager, she formed a close bond to an uncle on her father's side after discovering that he was a spiritualist. On her mother's side, there was Aunt Valle who was psychic. Sandra's mother also had the ability to read people, which she often did for friends and relatives. These relationships sparked Sandra to enter a more fully spiritual world as a teenager.

Sandra came into her own as a clairvoyant and a psychic during her time working as a stewardess. While on a trip to Hawaii, she shared a room with another stewardess and, quite suddenly, began to "read" her roommate — accurate information just started pouring out of her. That was Sandra's first inclination that she was gifted as a psychic, and ever since then she has accepted the role of service with open arms.

Sandra is able to see and commune with spirits, and whenever she goes back to England, she visits old castles with the hopes of interacting with the ghosts there. Once, while on one of her castle visits, she asked the tour guide if she could go into an antechamber that called her attention. The guide, after considering the unusual request, granted her permission, and Sandra went into what turned out to be a palatial dining room that had been closed for years.

Once inside, she saw the ghost of a manor lord leaning against the mantle of a large fireplace. The expression on his face said, "What are you doing in MY dining room?" He was dressed in Charles Dickens era clothing and was all business with Sandra; he then walked through a closed door and disappeared. The dining room felt "cold with an atmosphere of being watched." Sandra later learned from the tour guide that the castle's owner, now in Spirit, was often seen walking through the front door around tea time!

I asked Sandra what she thought the afterlife looked and felt like, and she replied, "There are green fields, lush valleys, and people are restored to perfect health. Part of being in spirit is to be healed of the illnesses you suffer during your earthly existence. In spirit, you can pick the age you wish to experience, usually the prime of your life. Like any part of earthly living, spirits are assigned tasks to do and, although you have free will, participation in these tasks is part of being in Spirit. All animosities of Earth are dissipated — jealousies, angers, rivalries, and hatreds are gone! You are cleansed of everything that we might call negative on Earth. It is almost as though you have a clean slate, ready to begin anew in another incarnation".

Sandra says that she is not afraid to die. For her, there is no death, and the fear that people experience is unfounded; more a fear of the unknown. She explains that we are all attached to the Earth by a silver cord. When our time to die comes, spirits gather around to escort us, and quickly sever the cord. Our soul is our essence and when we physically die, the soul flies around and goes up to Spirit. The soul is the part of us that lives on forever.

Three weeks after I interviewed Sandra Redman, I was sitting in the dining area of a Whole Foods in Edgewater, New Jersey having breakfast with a couple of friends. At 8:30 am, we were the only people there. From the corner of my eye, I saw a woman come in and sit about twenty feet from us. Then, I noticed that an employee politely approached and asked her to sit somewhere else because she needed to dress the windows by her table. She removed herself, and of all the available tables, she chose the one next to ours. The woman, whose name I later learned was Kathy, finished her breakfast, and, instead of leaving, turned around and came over to my table.

Kathy handed me her business card saying that she had overheard us talking about spiritual contact and life after death, and wondered if I would help her find a reliable medium. She had just lost her son in a tragic motorcycle accident and was heartbroken and in severe emotional pain. I took her card and promised I would find a medium for her that very day.

I called Sandra Redman, asked her to help, and without skipping a beat, she told me that Kathy's son had made his mother change seats at breakfast so she could overhear the conversation. Sandra went on to say that he was using me, in a loving way, to get in touch with his mother.

Within two weeks, Kathy was sitting in Sandra's office for a reading. Doug, her son, came through and was able to give his mother the message he had been wanting to give her ever since his untimely death. Kathy was deeply touched by the contact and, as a result, experienced a sense of peace and a significant amount of healing.

SPIRITUAL LIFE FELLOWSHIP, INC.

"The time will come ...when the effect on the heart will be to
bring all men to believe on God, on Love, and on Progress,
without any subdivisions, without any shades or distinctions..."
Lord Francis Bacon (Delivered through the mediumship
of Dr. George Dexter.)

There are many groups around the country that meet to connect with Spirit.
Some are basically meditation groups while others are mediumistic in nature
and call upon spirits to be present and lend their assistance. The Spiritual Life
Fellowship is one such group holding monthly meetings in Ridgefield, New
Jersey. I joined them one evening in June.

Rev. Barbara greeted me and introduced the group by saying that it "serves
both worlds," the spiritual and the physical, and that the meetings are based on
seven principles and no Bible. The premise of their work is that we are Spirit in
a physical body. Their purpose is to reunite us with the spirits of our loved ones
who have passed away.

There were sixteen participants, including Rev. Barbara and three other
mediums. The audience consisted mostly of women — I was one of only three
men in attendance. A candle was lighted, prayers were given, a song was sung,

and the meeting was ready to begin. Rev. Barbara and the other mediums gave readings and relayed messages to those in attendance, giving demonstrations by asking if anyone connected to what they were saying.

The connections made brought tears of sadness and joy as the mediums called out what they received from Spirit. Several of those assembled made contact with the spirits of those close to them and left the meeting filled with peace and a sense of knowing.

SPIRITUALIST CHURCH OF NEW YORK CITY - WHERE CITY AND MEDITATION MEET

"The only journey is the journey within."

Rainer Maria Rilke

"Spirit remains nameless in its true essence. Identification gives birth to separation, a sense of distinction as to what is, and what is not. It creates IT and its counterparts. To give Spirit an identification, in a sense, it is as if we are defining its perimeter. How could we possibly contain something that is so inclusive and expansive?"

Seiko L. Obayashi

On a warm evening in July, I visited the Sunday services of the Spiritualist Church of New York City. The church is located in a residential neighborhood on the east side of mid-town Manhattan. The inside is cozy, with high ceilings, and an altar decorated in a simple motif. The twenty-five or so congregants seemed to feel at ease and very much at home there.

The service I attended was focused on healing. An officer of the organization opened with a simple prayer followed by a song and a few church announcements. Then, the president of the Spiritualist Church, Seiko L. Obayashi, gave a ten-minute talk about healing and about all of us being part of the Oneness of the Universe. She explained "miracles can happen" at any time in our lives once we clear the obstructions that lie before us. She defined a miracle as "something supernatural not governed by the laws of nature." Whereas we are all participants in this reality, at the same time we are co-creating with God. Like Jesus taught, "I am one of you. You can do what I do."

There were four healers present at this service. All participants were invited to come up to the altar, sit in a chair in front of one of the healers, and allow a healing to take place. I intuitively chose a lady named Barbara Dominick, an ordained minister living in the Bronx. Rev. Barbara exuded love and tenderness as I watched her work on several people. When it was my turn, she gently gave me a healing that made my energy shift from fast paced to calm, which was exactly what I needed at that moment. I asked Barbara if she could give absent healing to a friend in hospital and she agreed wholeheartedly.

Afterwards, Barbara told me that her motto is, "You are the Infinite Light of One Love!" Because I wanted to know more about the service, Rev. Barbara, and what she did, I asked her for an explanation of her work. She answered, "When we detach from our attachments and release the fear based illusions we begin to step into the Light of our Divinity."

After the service, I was also able to speak to one of the regulars, Hector Santiago from New Jersey. He said that he had been attending the services for some time, and that he was participating in their minister-training program and expected to be ordained within a few months. I asked him what benefits he got from attending the services and what his definition of Spirit was, but he answered by simply stating that "in the beginning and in the end, what really matters is love. It is the most powerful feeling, the most noble, the most beautiful and the highest frequency." Love was evident, indeed, all throughout the service, and the congregants were ready to show kindness and love to one another. The gathering had been less about religion and more about our personal connection with Spirit.

Immediately after the service, we were all invited to go upstairs for a séance conducted by two ladies well-versed in such work. We were nineteen people sitting in a circle with the purpose of making contact with our loved ones in Spirit. I was intrigued by the idea having never attended a séance before.

The lights were dimmed and two candles burned on a table in the center of the room. We sat along with the two conductors, and after a brief silent meditation the séance got underway. One of the mediums pointed at someone in the circle and asked permission to approach her. Once there, she described a man of a certain age who had a message of hope and encouragement for her.

After five minutes communicating with that person, she went to a second person, asked permission, and delivered a message of a business nature from an aged aunt. It seems that the person being addressed was involved in a financial investment, and Spirit wanted to provide guidance in the right direction.

Then, it was my turn. I gave permission and my reading began with a message from my father. He wanted to give me love and blessings, and admonished me with, "Do not take things so seriously, have fun." — wise advice from a Spirit who knew me well.

The séance concluded after nearly everyone had gotten a message or advice of some sort. It was amazing to watch these two ladies point to people and, time after time, give accurate messages filled with valuable information. All of the messages, although at times stern, had one thing in common — love.

SWAMI ASOKANANDA - THE REMOVER OF SORROW

"Truth is one, paths are many."

Mahatma Gandi

I met Swami Asokananda at his ashram, the Integral Yoga Institute in New York City. I arrived with my long-time friend, Joe Brennan, who had made all the arrangements necessary for this meeting to take place. We were immediately led into the family room on the fourth floor where a looping recording of the most beautiful chanting I had ever heard created a friendly and welcoming atmosphere.

As Joe and I waited, we could smell food being prepared in the kitchen. People started drifting in, one by one, in anticipation of lunch, and soon thirteen advanced yoga students had joined us and were engaging us in quiet conversation. One of them, wearing a "Don't Worry, Be Happy" t-shirt, hearing that I was writing a book and was there to interview the Swami, asked me about the topic of my book. The moment I said that I was writing about our connections to our loved ones in Spirit, it was as if I had opened the door for them to share their own particular stories on the subject. A woman talked about losing her baby at birth and the feelings that accompany such an experience. Another spoke about her mother's passing and how it had affected her to the core of her being.

After lunch, the receptionist took me up in a private elevator to meet Swami Asokananda. Dressed in orange from head to toe, he greeted me with a broad smile and escorted me into the small 10' x 10' room where he spends most of his time. It had a bed, a writing desk, and a window overlooking a busy street. I had been told to greet him as "Swami Ji," so I did. I had the feeling of being in a place of peace with a man who reflected that peace in his inner being.

Swami Asokananda was raised in a non-religious Jewish family in Queens, New York. At the age of seventeen, he and a friend went on a cross-country road trip that would change the course of his life. While in California, he wandered into a bookstore and was drawn to a book entitled *Reincarnation*. He sheepishly admitted to stealing the book in order to read it. The material it contained had a lasting effect on him.

At nineteen, he moved into a yoga center and started the process of becoming a monk in the Hindu tradition. By the time he turned twenty-three, and after having experienced an overwhelming awakening to his life, he was a full fledged Swami intrigued by the concepts of reincarnation, celibacy, and all the other beliefs taught by his tradition. His new name was Swami Asokananda, meaning "the remover of sorrow." *Sok* means worry, sorrow, or anxiety, and *a* means to remove. *Anda* is the traditional yogic name ending meaning bliss.

"Following such a lifestyle," Swami Ji says, "you must be aware and willing to face the repercussions of your actions. Life is a long and winding road where we both regularly finish old karma and start new karma."

I was most interested in his view of Spirit, and Swami Ji gave me a clear definition when he said, "Spirit is one consciousness that flows through everything." He went on further to say that "many people need to see Spirit through an image or icon" because they "need something to feel connected to God." His beliefs tell him that "Spirit transcends religion," and that when you relax through meditation your "sensory organs get in touch with something peaceful — being with Spirit in this state is a home-free feeling." Swami Ji calmly told me that "we are Spirit and one consciousness; we are the whole body of Spirit and not a cell." To him, talking about spiritual things is "beyond the mental realm."

Swami Ji feels there is much misunderstanding about religion and is befuddled by the existence of so-called "spiritual wars" where each side prays to

God to kill those on the other side. He laughed at the ridiculousness of such a way of thinking.

Swami Ji follows a daily yogic spiritual practice that includes five of the yamas (non-injury, truthfulness, non-stealing, Divine conduct, compassion, honesty, patience, steadfastness, moderate attitude and parity) and five of the niyamas (remorse, contentment, giving faith, worship, scripture reading, cognition, sacred vows, recitation and austerity). The yamas and niyamas are the foundation and ethical guidelines of yoga.

One must still the mind, and both meditation and yoga are ways to accomplish that. He explains that yoga is, in fact, a way of meditation. By stilling the mind, you get closer to who you are and in doing so you get closer to God. He recommends that we constantly "observe the mind." To maintain a state of mindfulness, he performs his meditation practice three times a day.

About our spirits and reincarnation, Swami Ji says, "Everybody dies and nobody dies," meaning that we are born again and again, through reincarnation, into new bodies and in new places. I asked him who decides how we come back and whom we reincarnate as, and he explained that it was "the Intelligence that knows what each soul needs to move on."

Swami Ji says that a good example of reincarnation can be seen in the film *Heaven Can Wait*. Produced in 1978, it tells the story of a professional football player who loses his life and is reincarnated, first into the body of a billionaire and then into that of an athlete. The film illustrates how we are escorted from one lifetime to another and that there is a plan for each of us.

Swami Ji also stresses that there is a strong energy behind thought forms, so we must make sure to send good thoughts to everyone all the time. He emphasizes the fact that God sends people to "rub and scrub us."

TOM CRATSLEY - AN AGENT OF GROWTH AND CHANGE

"It is love that holds everything together and it is the Everything also."

Rumi

Tom Cratsley is the associate director of the Lily Dale Spiritual School of Healing and Prophesy. Lily Dale, neatly tucked into the western border of New York State, is an energetically special place and Tom, widely known and greatly respected in healing circles around the world, is a perfect fit for it. In addition to being the associate director of the school, he also teaches and performs spiritual healing, calling himself an agent of growth and change. He defines himself as an "agent of change" rather than as a healer because, as he freely admits, he has "no idea how healing takes place."

Tom was first drawn to spiritual healing when he was nineteen and living in Buffalo, New York. His number one mentor was Edith Wendling, a pioneer in the modern field of healing who lived to be over a hundred years old. In the 1970s, Tom began to serve at the Lily Dale temple; the largest center for spiritualism in the world.

As a result of all his experience in the field of healing, Tom has developed a technique he calls *Restructuring.* In *Restructuring,* he helps his clients find the core trauma that has led them to dis-ease, so they can then proceed to release the emotions attached to their conditions — in releasing the emotions behind the disease, the healing takes place.

Tom believes that all healing is self-healing. Healing comes from a shift in consciousness produced by letting go of old assumptions. This letting go leaves us free to heal since what was keeping the dis-ease in place was our holding on to the patterns that first brought it about. He explains, "Trauma holds on because people feel they are helpless — the trauma becomes buried in the sub-consciousness. *Restructuring* is very effective because it stops patterns."

As an example of his work, Tom remembers helping a woman in her sixties who was suffering from back problems. Through the process of *Restructuring,* he was able to discover that his client had been wounded in the back during a past life and had carried the wounds into her present reality. Once the woman identified all the emotions associated with the back wound, the pain went away.

Another case was that of a man whose business dealings had gone bad after the betrayal of a business partner. Through *Restructuring,* Tom brought this man back to a past life where the original betrayal had occurred. He discovered that in that life the man had not only been betrayed, but also killed by his partner. When these patterns were cleared, the man regained his passion for business and enjoyed successful enterprises once again.

When a person's level of frustration reaches a certain point, an unveiling of the truth takes place that can bring about a healing. In such cases, Tom refers to himself as a "witness to healing." He feels that "God or the Universe and the person being healed do the healing."

Tom is appreciative of the power of God. One of his past lives revealed him as a sound healer in ancient Egypt, but this time around he has concentrated on working with the elementals — the consciousness in all substances that programs them to do what they are supposed to do.

Tom Cratsley's overall philosophy of healing can be summed up in a few words: "Healing is an aspect of evolution. Every time you go through a healing process our consciousness grows in some way and that allows the species to grow. The nature of God is evolution. God is an evolving God and everything is potential healing."

CONCLUSION

Spirit Lives! has taken me on a magnificently rewarding two and a half year journey of research, interviewing, and writing. You could argue that the journey started with my childhood experiences of the unexplained "knowingness" exhibited by my grandfather, but whenever you mark the beginning; it has brought me to fascinating places and people.

Most of the people who crossed my path along the way were fully aware of their connections to Spirit. As a result, they allowed me to publish their stories as illustrations of their beliefs about life after physical death. They exposed their innermost feelings about the subject; feelings that for some were a hidden, private facet of their lives. In fact, many were relieved to finally be telling their stories about being touched by Spirit. For them, it was a catharsis of sorts.

Approximately half of the people I interviewed were professional psychics, mediums, or clairvoyants who do this work every day. The others were so called "ordinary" people who had had "extraordinary" experiences that they were now ready to share. The book is a celebration of Spirit and of the infinite ways in which it interacts with us in our daily lives.

I set out on this journey to confirm a belief I held all my life. The belief that life exists in Spirit before we incarnate and continues after we leave this physical plane. In effect, there is no death in the sense that we have been taught to believe — death does not exist from the perspective of the soul. I was determined to share with my readers the knowledge of the eternal nature of life. I wanted to help them perceive life from a different point of view; a point of view that would launch them on their own journeys into a more loving and forgiving nature.

I entered this quest with an open mind willing to hear dissident voices and consider both sides of the argument only to discover that a strong preponderance of the people were actually "believers." Even those who had no particular hard evidence declared they were leading their lives with the conviction that life in spirit continues after physical death. It was not their religion that convinced them, but an inner feeling.

Throughout this journey, I was amazed to encounter so many people with a deep interest in the afterlife. I recall one day in December 2011 when I was a guest speaker at the local Rotary Club. The Rotarians sat in polite attention while I spoke about my first book, *Thinking In English*, but came fully alive when I began to talk about this book, which was in the beginning stages at the time. During the question and answer period following my talk, all the questions had to do with spirituality. One of the participants even made me promise that I would let her know the moment this book was published. That kind of enthusiasm made me realize that this information is thirsting in people's hearts.

While speaking before another service organization in the spring of 2012, I could almost touch the interest of the audience. At the conclusion of my talk, the president approached me and said, "authors usually put our members to sleep, but the topic of your speech brought them fully to life. I have never seen our members so excited."

Spirit Lives! taught me much about people's reactions to Spirit and, as a result, about my own feelings in this area. Writing this book allowed me to expand the notion I had of myself as a spiritual being allowing me to recognize my dual citizenships in both the physical world and the world of Spirit. In some ways, it opened me even more to the fact that we are spiritual beings in physical, earthly bodies. Even in the reactions from the skeptics I met, I felt a longing to see more than a one-life existence and a yearning to make more sense of life. Many of them seemed frustrated that there was nothing they could see beyond this one lifetime.

Writing this book also reinforced in me the idea of following my intuition. When we follow our intuition, that deep feeling of inner truth, we are never led astray. I have made it a habit to act according to the information I glean from my inner guidance, from my nightly meditations, and from the hints the world around me offers like when a friend recommended that I turn my meditations into a book on spiritual life. In all cases, when I look back, I am happy to have been shown the way.

The journey of this book fed my thirst to know more about Spirit, and in doing so, it showed me more about my own self. The "more" that I was shown gave me a greater compassion for myself and for those around me. It led me to see that some of the conflicts in this life may well emanate from karmic threads originating in previous times, but that no matter their origin, their resolution is always to be found in love — love for myself and for those to whom the karmic threads connect me. Not seeking a resolution in this life would only cause the karma to continue, thus prolonging the conflict.

Throughout the writing process, I was able to both observe and experience the incredible power of the love we have inside. Love is the most powerful emotion available and it always wins out. Many of the professionals interviewed agreed that the most direct way to deal with conflict was by loving. In doing so, growth is assured.

Another important lesson was to see how religions sometimes keep us narrow in our thinking. Those who follow strict religious dogmas may not wish to expand outside of what they have been taught to believe. To believe in a spiritual existence means that we eagerly and bravely go beyond the guidelines established by our religious teachings. We think *outside the box* and open ourselves to a magical world previously unknown to us. The choice is ours. Some find this forbidding or disturbing, but for others it can be exciting and exhilarating. I have chosen the latter path in my life and, in choosing that path, can see the Oneness in us all.

In researching and writing this book, I have learned that there are many spiritual groups around the world that meet regularly to give spiritual readings to whomever asks for guidance. Many of these groups have memberships, but most allow the public to walk in as freely as they wish for a reading.

There is also the growing recognition of the presence of Spirit through television shows that instantly increase awareness of spirituality and provide a platform for discussion. Personalities such as Louise L. Hay and Dr. Wayne Dyer present their ideas of spirit on PBS as well as on CDs and DVDs.

In many ways, this book wrote itself, in that one paragraph developed into the next rather smoothly and one chapter gave birth to another in a natural sort of way. There were many times when the manuscript would not allow me to put it down and take a break — it called out to me to keep on writing.

Throughout the writing process, I found myself being introduced to all sorts of people who either had a story to tell or who would introduce me to someone who had a positive contribution to make to the book. I was continuously being guided to those who would add to the whole experience.

This book has given me a once in a lifetime opportunity to look at spirit through the eyes of professionals and ordinary people who have had their lives changed; each time I witnessed something new, it magnified my own experiences. I would not change these two and a half years for anything in the world. And, most importantly, *Spirit Lives!* has allowed me to spread the word of the magnificent aspect of life that is the world of spirit where all our dead friends and relatives reside and where we all shall also be one day — a world where love is the abiding climate and acceptance of all is the norm.

APPENDICES

DEATH

Most of us live our lives in fear of death and dying, dreading the entire notion of death and the aura which surrounds it. We associate it with loss and do not want to lose anything, particularly loved ones. We put the body of the dead away and out of sight. We bury, entomb, or, more dramatically, cremate them, and then either hold their ashes in a container or sprinkle them over a favorite spot. Furthermore, we "paint" the dead bodies using make-up, fancy clothing, and hairdos, so that observers will say, "He looks so good, almost as though he were alive!" How could he look good? He is dead! But, yet, in the face of such insane behavior, we do that. Cold death is too strong for us to digest. We marinate death, so we can chew and absorb it into our consciousness. Death, in our culture, is never taken raw like sushi.

Most funeral ceremonies in our American culture are solemn, sad events. We wear the customary black with tears flowing like waterfalls. In very few religions do we see happiness in facing death. One such exception, in the modern industrialized world, is the Baptist faith where celebrants call the funeral a "homecoming" and hymns of rejoicing are sang because the passing means their loved one has gone back home to God. It is a happy occasion and it is celebrated without mourning. This type of ceremony loudly proclaims that death is not a sad event because the departed one is now with God, and in stating that, it also lets us know that death does not mean the end, but only the transfer to a spiritual life that is as lively as the physical life we lead, if not more.

The stigma of death equaling loss is deeply ingrained in our consciousness. Death is nothing like what we have been conditioned to think, you might say it is only a transfer from a life on Earth to a life in Spirit. You go from one location to another; it is the same stream of life, but on another level of consciousness. The important point to embrace is that both Earth life and the Spiritual life are existence. Spirit-life is simply existence on a plain that is invisible to us "Earth bound" people — invisible to some, at least. People who have developed their gift of mediumship can normally interact with the spirits of those we refer to as dead.

If for only a moment we could think of Spiritual life as being as real as the physical life we perceive through our senses, our perspective of life would change dramatically and widen miraculously. We would suddenly see ourselves and our Universe as being radically different from the way we see it now. The practice of some cultures to revere their elderly and their ancestors might become common practice around the world. Respect and reverence for all life might become the norm instead of the exception. As Dr. Wayne Dyer says, "When you change the way you look at things, the things you look at change."

But for now, most Americans equate death with a final ending, and more needs to be done to bring to the foreground of our consciousness the inspiration, the heart, and the courage necessary to break with the equation of death = loss. Once this is accomplished, more of us will begin to think of death as a "homecoming" to the loving arms of our Creator, the Infinite One.

THE GROWING INTEREST IN THE PAST LIVES PHENOMENON

What would you think and how would you feel if you were sure that life existed after physical death? What would your reaction be if you could see the after death experience and interpret it as comfortable and welcoming? What would it mean for you if you had the certainty that the experience "in between" lifetimes was a good, positive one? How would that make you feel about life and death? How would you feel about physical existence?

Many who have gone through near death experiences (NDEs), and have reported on them, have had very reassuring words about what lies beyond the so-called "white light" that seems to serve as a "bridge" between realities. In fact, highly respected medical doctors have written on this subject and illustrated their findings with first hand examples provided by their patients or research subjects. Many of these stories echo each other in terms of the themes that run through them and the way in which they give us eyewitness accounts of life after death. Some near death experiences are so pleasurable and peaceful that the people involved report wanting to remain "dead" instead of coming back to this plane of existence.

If all the questions of what happens after our physical death had reassuring, warm answers, would you lead your life differently? One of the greatest fears we have while on Earth is the fear of death and dying. If we were sure that death and dying were a wonderful experience and that our family and friends are not gone, would we welcome it as just another integral part of life? The mystique surrounding death has befuddled man from time immemorial. To free ourselves of such anguish would be akin to medical science finding a simple cure for a devastating disease. At the very least, it would be a mind-expanding opportunity.

Spiritualism has enjoyed great popularity in this country during certain periods of history, but during the last 50 years, Americans have shown a growing interest in learning more about past lives and the entire notion of past life regression. Many renowned experts have published books on the subject. In 1988, Dr. Brian Weiss, a Yale educated psychiatrist, wrote the best-selling *Many Lives, Many Masters*. This book's publication caused a major shift in the way the subject of past lives is perceived in this country. It opened our collective eyes to the age-old notion of living in Spirit during and after physical death demonstrating that we go on living in very identifiable ways.

Dr. Raymond Moody has also explored the life after death hypothesis in several of his books. He, too, is a medical doctor with years of experience and a wealth of respect. One of his best-known books is *Life After Life* in which he investigates the survival of bodily death. Dr. Moody is also considered an expert on near death experiences (NDEs) and has a wide following.

A more recent book, *Heaven Is For Real* (2010), details the story of a four-year-old boy named Colton who has a near death experience. Written by the boy's father, an ordained minister, it tells the story of how Colton died for about three minutes on account of a misdiagnosed illness. When he returned to life he was able to describe Heaven, Jesus, and the other inhabitants of Heaven, including his grandfather who had died three decades before Colton's birth and his own brother who had been stillborn. Colton's descriptions of Heaven bear a remarkable resemblance to those outlined in the Bible giving us pause to think about NDEs and the possibility of living somewhere else after physical death.

Bookstore shelves are packed with books on life after death, past live regression, and spiritualism. Barnes & Noble, for example, has an extensive section dedicated to Spiritualism with hundreds of titles for sale, and one just has to look at the endless variety of offerings on Amazon.com to recognize the immense popularity of this genre. Spiritualism as a topic of learning and exploration is not limited to traditional books; it also forms a big part of the e-book and audio book market, not to mention movies and television shows. People love the subject and are eager to learn more about it.

In the 1950's, during the early days of television, CBS aired a popular series called *Topper* with veteran actor Leo G. Carroll in the title role. *Topper* was the story of the vice president of a bank, Cosmo Topper and his dim-witted wife Henrietta, played by Lee Patrick. They buy a house from the estate of a young couple, George and Marion Kerby, who had been killed in a snow avalanche along with their dog, a St. Bernard named Neil. Soon after moving in, Cosmo realizes that the ghosts of George, Marion and Neil were haunting the house. Being the only one who can see and hear the ghosts, they cause Topper to be involved in all sorts of humorous adventures.

Topper aired on CBS from 1953 to 1955 for a total of 78 episodes. America loved *Topper* and tuned in every week. As a child, I watched it faithfully. It was a show ahead of its time and the first one to explore the notion of life after death. The main character was an intelligent and sophisticated banker, and the audience had no problem accepting the concept of people surviving physical death.

In pre-war 1941, Universal Studios produced the movie *Hold That Ghost* starring the comedy team of Abbott & Costello. *Hold That Ghost* blends comedy with the idea of the soul's survival after death. It remains hugely popular to this day as evidence by its availability on DVD as well as making part of the roster of movies offered by both Netflix and Blockbuster. Not bad for a low budget movie made over 70 years ago!

The subject of ghosts, spirits, and spirituality has a long history of success in Hollywood, with blockbusters like *Ghost* (1990) and *Titanic* (1997) drawing A-list actors, it shows how enthusiastically the general public responds to such themes.

In *Ghost*, Sam Wheat, played by Patrick Swayze, is killed during a botched mugging, but his love for his wife, played by Demi Moore, enables him to remain on Earth as a ghost in order to protect her from Carl Bruner, played by Tony Goldwyn, the man responsible for his death.

In *Titanic*, Jack Dawson, played by Leonardo DiCaprio lives on forever in the heart and mind of his young lover, Rose DeWitt Bukater, played by Kate Winslet — "Nothing on earth could come between them."

The 1999 movie *The Sixth Sense* starring Haley Joel Osment as a troubled nine-year-old boy, Cole Sear, and Bruce Willis as child psychologist Dr. Malcolm Crowe, centers around an isolated boy who confesses to seeing dead people. The now famous line, "I can see dead people" will linger long in the memories of theatregoers.

The Sixth Sense cost approximately $40 million to make and had a worldwide gross of over $600 million dollars. It was nominated for six Academy Awards including Best Picture, Best Director, Best Original Screenplay, Best Supporting Actor (Haley Joel Osment), Best Supporting Actress, and Best Editing. In addition to the Academy Awards, *The Sixth Sense* received many other awards from a host of associations in the fields of film, writing, science fiction, and horror. It remains a classic example of this genre.

Sometimes, Hollywood movies dealing with Spirit takes on a sinister tone. In the 2005 movie *Hide and Seek*, Robert DeNiro plays a widower who tries to piece together his life in the wake of his wife's suicide. His daughter, played by Dakota Fanning, finds solace in an imaginary friend, which turns out to be an evil spirit. Filled with mystery, murder, and suspicion, this is not your typical movie about a friendly ghost, but rather it portrays a dark side which American audiences love to hate.

In the autumn of 2010, Warner Brothers released *Hereafter*, a film directed and produced by Clint Eastwood and starring Matt Damon. It follows three parallel stories of people affected by death. Matt Damon is a blue-collar factory worker who has the gift of communicating with the dead, Cecile de France plays a television journalist living in France who lived through a tsunami and a near-death experience, and actor brothers Frankie and George McLaren play brothers, one of whom is hit and killed by a car. Set in San Francisco, Paris, and London, *Hereafter* is emotionally moving and effective in its portrayal of our relationship to Spirit.

Americans seem unable to stay away from films dealing with the afterlife or psychic phenomena. They seem to be almost critic-proof, and in most cases their success is assured.

On television, CBS had a huge hit in 2005 with *The Ghost Whisperer* starring Jennifer Love Hewitt. The show ran for five years, 107 episodes, with remarkable success, averaging 10 million viewers. The show featured Love-Hewitt as medium Melinda Gordon who had the ability to see and communicate with the spirits of the dead. While trying to live as normal a life as possible, Melinda helps earthbound spirits resolve their problems so that they can cross over into the Light and enter Heaven. Ghosts seek Melinda's help to relay messages to living loved ones or to help resolve situations that have kept them from reaching a state of peace. The show was based on the work of mediums James Van Praagh and Mary Ann Winkowski, both of whom worked on the production of the show.

It is part of the human psyche to be interested in the unknown, and life after life is the greatest of all unknowns. Over the millennia, man has sought to unravel this mystery. As a result, the NDE is the best way to ascertain the answer to the questions: is there life after life, and, if so, what is the nature of that life after life?

PAST LIFE REGRESSION

The rise in the practice of past life regression through hypnosis is one of the clearest indicators of the prevalent interest in accessing past life information. A great number of spiritually inclined therapists have adopted this method of treatment in an effort to resolve deep-seated obstructions in their clients' psyche. Regression serves this purpose by bringing to the surface valuable information relevant to the person's present life circumstances. Through regression sessions, people can find out why they are experiencing what they are experiencing since one of the tenets of this sort of treatment is that many situations in this life can be traced to episodes experienced in previous lives. Through "traveling in time," someone can find the missing piece that would let them unravel the hidden meaning behind present situations.

Through the journey of past life regression, patients can acquire insights into facets of their lives that might have previously appeared random. For example, someone might discover information to help explain why they are drawn to certain professions or the reasons why certain people treat them lovingly and others harshly. Past life regression is a way to see into the intricacies that form the patterns of our existence and as such, it can be the ultimate healing technique.

We come to this life with lessons to learn. Earth is a great classroom for learning the lessons needed to shift into a higher consciousness and planes of existence. In *The Power of the Spoken Word*, one of my favorite metaphysical writers,

Florence Scovel Shinn, wrote, "Nothing has ever come uninvited into your life." Physical impediments, challenging relationships, or even tragic "accidents" can come to teach us valuable lessons. We, however, do not have to wait a lifetime to have the puzzle solved for us, if we remain open-minded to learning more about the people and ourselves.

Other examples of past life challenges manifesting in someone's life could be poverty and homelessness. The homeless community of larger American cities has been steadily increasing. To consider that a person has chosen to be homeless is unthinkable to some, but should that be the case at a soul level, what would the lesson presented by homelessness be? Certainly, it must be said that the reasons behind our lives' circumstances are not always literal. To assume that a homeless person has to be going through a basic lesson in appreciation for home, family, self-respect, and dignity, shows a limited, literal understanding of what could simply be a means to reach and be with people that otherwise would not be accessible to that soul.

One thing is certain; all of us have lessons to learn in this life. If we accept this as true, learning can begin immediately. Asking "why me?" and fighting our circumstances will only serve to impede our progress and delay the inevitable learning.

Although the world of Spirit appears invisible to most people, it exerts a powerful influence on the world and on our individual lives. For those of us who cannot perceive Spirit, there are people skilled in this type of perception that can offer us assistance. They are able to feel the presence of Spirit through their five senses and their intuition. These people know that something is there with them. It is not necessary for them to physically see because they have a knowing.

As we progress into the twenty-first century, more and more people are adopting beliefs in the presence and the power of Spirit. Even among those who question, a growing number are at least open to consider the possibility of Spirit and of our lives in a spiritual world. Some cultures are more prone to believe in the reality of Spirit and embrace reincarnation and the presence of their departed ancestors as part of their daily lives. They need no urging to believe, they just live their lives with these truths. The belief in Spirit is an integral part of their lives and there is no room for questioning.

Cultures that are rooted in the belief in Spirit lead lives that are more serene and peaceful. They are convinced that life is everlasting and that one lifetime segues into the next with all that we learn from one life informing the life experience of the following one. Each new life brings with it the opportunity to explore a different gender, race, home location, and culture. This is the natural order of the Spirit; our souls are elevated through our living. These cultures see previous life experiences as stepping-stones and the current life as an agreement made between lives with the help of teachers and guides in Spirit.

When Spirit works through people to accomplish results, all aspects of our lives become fascinating. An example of this can be seen in miraculous cures of physical ailments, injuries and diseases. Sometimes, Spirit accomplishes these miracle cures through the use of human healers, and at other times the diseased person is able to bring about the healing through their faith and the strength of their belief.

Medical history is filled with stories of miracle cures where the terminally ill have gone on to live full and fulfilling lives way after the time allotted them by medical professionals. When we are able to see ourselves as Spirit, we can expect miracles to happen on a routine basis; there is nothing we cannot accomplish.

SOME CASES OF CONTACT
WITH SPIRIT

Many people report having seen, felt, or experienced the presence of those who have passed, and feel a definite closeness to those spirits who are near and always willing to enter their lives for support or to give answers to puzzling questions. Having discussed this topic with many people, I have placed their experiences in one of three categories: senders and receivers, receivers, or believers.

Senders and Receivers

First, and most spectacular, are people who actually see and are able to communicate with spirit. They have been given access to a special, magical world that some say is more alive than the so-called physical world in which we live. They are able to hear or sense spirits, and thus can, at will, establish mutually beneficial dialogues with them; they are both receivers and senders. Some people in this category are mediums and dedicate their professional lives to this kind of work. Others are what I call accidental mediums in that they do not choose this life, but are selected by Spirit to serve in this capacity.

Some mediums in this first group must go into a deep trance in order to contact spirits, while others are able to establish completely conscious connections without the necessity of trance work.

Receivers

In the second category are those who have the ability to hear, feel, or sense spirit, but are not able to communicate back and establish a coherent dialogue — they are receivers. They can perceive Spirit's guidance and intuitively know what to do, but are not able to actually interact with the concrete energies of the Spirit world.

Receivers usually experience spirits through meditation. They hear their subtle voices, are able to identify them, and feel real attachment to the spirits with which they communicate.

Believers

People who believe in the reality of spirit, but have not yet experienced direct contact form this third category. They might read material on the subject, talk to like-minded friends, and watch television programs, but the Spirit world remains for them a matter of faith and intellect.

Believers know that Spirit exists, but cannot illustrate their beliefs with concrete examples. At times, they may exhibit a degree of doubt, but they inherently know that life goes on after death. Most of them profess not to *need* empirical proof; cherishing the concept that Spirit exists somewhere out there in the great Beyond.

All of the world's largest religions believe in life after death, and teach it as one of their central tenets. In some, Hinduism and Buddhism for example, life's issues and challenges are explained through the process of reincarnation. The difficulties of this life are believed to have been brought about by our choices and actions in previous lives. Therefore, it is our responsibility to correct those difficulties in order to free the remainder of this life, and subsequent lives, to be filled with joy and happiness.

DR. GARY E. SCHWARTZ -
SPIRIT AND SCIENCE

"I believe that science . . . can potentially help increase our
ability to receive spiritual information accurately, and we can
then act upon it safely and wisely."

Dr. Gary E. Schwartz

What does science say about the idea of life after death and the world of Spirit?
Gary E. Schwartz, Ph.D. fearlessly faced this question. Dr. Schwartz is a professor of psychology at the University of Arizona and the director of its Human
Energy Systems Laboratory. He received his doctorate from Harvard University
and served as professor of psychology at Yale. He has published more than four
hundred scientific papers and edited eleven academic books. In his book, *The
Afterlife Experiments: Breakthrough Scientific Evidence of Life After Death*, Dr. Schwartz
explores the existence of Spirit through strict scientific experimentation; that is,
he follows the principles and protocols of science to examine the ethereal possibilities of communicating with Spirit.

Dr. Schwartz and his research partner Dr. Linda G. Russek devised some
ingenious experiments geared towards proving or disproving the existence of life

after death. Risking criticism from the scientific community, they asked promi-
nent American mediums to take part in the experiments. The group of mediums
included John Edward, Suzane Northrup, Laurie Campbell, Suzy Smith, and
George Anderson, to name a few. Under controlled laboratory conditions, the
mediums attempted to access information from the physically dead friends and
relatives of "sitters." The sitters, both men and women, were hidden from view
and not allowed to speak in order to prevent the mediums from having any facial
or auditory clues.

The mediums addressed a variety of subjects and received messages covering a wide range of information; from details of a son's suicide, to a man's doubts
about life after death, to the forecast of a spouse's death. The results obtained
caused Dr. Schwartz to reconsider his own personal skepticism and led him to
make some startling conclusions. The book reads like a novel, but the results are
non-fictional, scientific conclusions.

Parts of the experiments were aired on HBO in a documentary that employed
multiple mediums to get information from a single sitter. Prior to being read, the
sitters had completed extensive questionnaires about their losses and various
life experiences. Dr. Schwartz went to great lengths to prevent the possibility of
fraud, error, or statistical coincidence.

The experiments were divided according to the criteria they included. In *The
Miraval Silent-Sitter Experiment*, for example, four mediums and ten sitters participated. The experiment consisted of two sessions, one where the sitters were
silent and invisible and the other in which sitters were allowed "yes" and "no"
answers. *The Canyon Ranch Totally Silent Sitter Experiment* involved three mediums
and five silent sitters. *The White Crow* experiments used three sitters with Laurie
Campbell as the medium. After all the data was collected and analyzed, the evidence of life after death was overwhelming.

These experiments clearly demonstrate that mediums can successfully establish contact and receive information from spiritual sources. Given the impec-
cability of Dr. Schwartz's reputation, neither questions nor doubts can be raised
regarding the methods followed. Dr. Schwartz is not a young doctor attempting
to make a name by being involved in controversial experiments. His credentials
were well established and his name widely recognized in scientific circles by the
time the experiments were performed.

This line of inquiry was initially motivated by Dr. Russek's feelings for her
departed father. Dr. Russek often spoke about his passing and her deep love for

him. Hearing her express her longing for her father prompted Dr. Schwartz to come up with an experimental protocol aimed at proving that her father's soul continued to live in Spirit after his physical death.

Dr. Schwartz concludes his study by posing the question, "how would the knowledge that our loved ones are conducting their lives elsewhere in spirit change our daily lives?" He imagines that it would give us permission to slow down, since in this new paradigm life would be endless, and whatever we did not achieve in one lifetime could be achieved in another.

The *living soul hypothesis*, as Dr. Schwartz calls it, causes us to pause and question our love and kindness towards each other and ourselves in this present life. It also makes us question the consequences of living with this new realization. How would you feel if you were cruel to someone who then dies, and you knew that that person was still very much alive in spirit? How would you react if it were a scientifically proven fact? Would it make you think twice before you acted against others? Would that knowledge, in effect, prompt you to treat others differently while you were both on Earth?

Dr. Schwartz presents a view of the oneness of all. The notion that what we do has eternal effects may change the way we look at life and death. If it changes our thinking, and we start to look at others as one with ourselves, we may be a giant step closer to achieving everlasting peace on Earth.

EBEN ALEXANDER, M.D. -
"PROOF OF HEAVEN"

"Consciousness is the most profound mystery in the Universe."
Eben Alexander, M.D.

The October 2012 issue of *Newsweek* featured a fascinating cover story on Dr. Eben Alexander's visit to Heaven. Dr. Alexander is an accomplished American neurosurgeon who in the fall of 2008 suffered a seizure that left him in a coma for seven days. The seizure began with a severe headache and concluded with his entire cerebral cortex shutting down. His doctors believed that he had contracted bacterial meningitis and gave him a slim chance of survival beyond a vegetative state.

While his body lay in a coma, his mind was very much alive. As the bacteria attacked the cortex, his consciousness traveled to what he describes as "another, larger dimension of the universe." He went on to say that in that dimension "we are much more than our brains and bodies." Dr. Alexander now feels that "death is not the end of consciousness, but rather a chapter in a vast and incalculably positive journey."

Dr. Alexander does not claim to have been the first to discover "that consciousness exists beyond the body." But he does state that, as far as he knows, no one before him has done so "while their cortex was completely shut down." In effect, Dr. Alexander had inhabited a level of consciousness during his coma.

He witnessed a "place of clouds" that "showed up sharply against the deep blue-black sky." Above the clouds he saw "flocks of transparent, shimmering beings arced across the sky, leaving long, streamer-like lines behind them." These beings were different from anything Dr. Alexander had ever seen and made a sound "like a glorious chant" as a means of expressing their joy. The sound was "palpable and almost material, like a rain that you can feel on your skin but doesn't get you wet." He felt they represented "higher forms" of existence.

Dr. Alexander thought that everything "was distinct, yet everything was also part of everything else, like the rich and intermingled designs on a Persian carpet . . . or a butterfly's wing."

He felt the presence of a woman and was able to describe her in detail: young, with high cheekbones, deep-blue eyes, and golden brown hair that framed a lovely face. He saw himself riding on the "wing of a butterfly" with this woman. As a matter of fact, there were millions of butterflies around them forming "a river of life and color, moving through the air." He sums up his experience with this female presence with the words, "She looked at me with a look that, if you saw it for five seconds, would make your whole life up to that point worth living, no matter what had happened in it so far. It was not a romantic look. It was not a look of friendship. It was a look that was somehow beyond all these, beyond all the different compartments of love we have down here on Earth. It was something higher, holding all those other kinds of love within itself while at the same time being much bigger than all of them."

Her three part message was: "You are loved and cherished, dearly, forever," "you have nothing to fear," and "there is nothing you can do wrong."

He entered an "immense void, completely dark, infinite in size, yet also infinitely comforting." He refers to the universe as "a giant cosmic womb" — a dark place "full to brimming with light."

Dr. Alexander's explanation is that "there is no true separation" in the universe. He is now determined to spend the rest of his life investigating "the true nature of consciousness," and the fact that we are "more, much more than our physical brains."

ABOUT THE AUTHOR

Dr. John B. Muciaccia was a high school English teacher and Vice-Principal in the Palisades Park, New Jersey Public School System. There, he was the founder and sponsor of the *Famous People Program*, which achieved national recognition on several television programs and a feature article in *The New York Times*. In 2010, he published *Thinking In English*, which outlines his unique method of teaching English to foreign-born adults. *Spirit Lives!* is his second book; an exploration of his life-long interest in Spirit.

Dr. Muciaccia resides in Hoboken, New Jersey where he is working on an upcoming project. He may be reached at www.drjohnmuciaccia.com.

CONTACT INFORMATION

Agota Repka: AgiHealing@gmail.com

Braco: www.Braco.net

Brianne Leslie: Ceremoniesrev@gmail.com

David Meredith: Bodywork1@optonline.net

Eben Alexander, M.D.: www.Lifebeyonddeath.net

Erich Heineman: Erich@deepvisioning.com

Frank St. James: F.St.James70@gmail.com

Gandharva Sauls: www.yourlifeblueprint.net

Dr. Gary E. Schwartz: www.drgaryschwartz.com

John of God: www.JohnOfGod.com

Lindsey Sass: Website: www.lindseyheartsoflight.com
E-mail: LindseySass@hotmail.com

Lynn Hambro: www.ArtofHealingLMH.com

Michael Charney: Salesworks@aol.com

Michael Zaikowski: Michael@Thepracticalmagi.com

Nicole Miller: Thetempley1@aol.com

Red Duke: Mysticred@ymail.com

Roger Ansanelli: www.RogerAnsanelli.com

Roland Comtois: Rcomtois.newsletter@gmail.com

Ryan Michaels: Psychicryan.com

Sandra Redman: Sredman560@aol.com

Spiritual Life Fellowship Inc.: info@spirituallifefellowship.org

Spiritual Church of New York City: SpiritChurchNYC@aol.com

Swami Asokananda: asokananda@IYINY.org

Tom Cratsley: Tomcratsley.com